Strategic Planning
for School Managers

Strategic Planning for School Managers

A Handbook of Approaches to
Strategic Planning and Development
for Schools and Colleges

Jim Knight

KOGAN
PAGE

London • Stirling (USA)

First published in 1997

Kogan Page Limited
120 Pentonville Road
London N1 9JN
and
22883 Quicksilver Drive
Stirling, VA 20166, USA

© Jim Knight, 1997

British Library Cataloguing in Publication Data

A CIP record for this book is available from the British Library.

ISBN 0 7494 1726 9

Typeset by Kogan Page
Printed and bound in Great Britain by Clays Ltd, St Ives plc

Contents

The Case for Strategic Planning

This handbook has been written with the intention of helping school leaders in all kinds and sizes of schools and colleges with the management part of their job that relates to the strategic development of their organisations. It seeks to put before its readers a series of practical models from which school leaders can derive:

- some insights into the fundamental nature of strategy and its development, and
- approaches to the process of planning to achieve that development.

However, before coming to the first of these models/approaches, I wish to raise some issues that relate to the phrase commonly used to describe this whole process and which provides the title for this book – 'strategic planning'. I believe that, in terms of the mental models it conjures up in the minds of those who use it, it is very frequently misconstrued. As a result the process actually carried out and, more importantly, the consequences which flow from it, can only rarely be properly described as strategic. The problem is the usual, twofold one of the words themselves and the way they are interpreted. As Tennyson observed, 'words, like Nature, half reveal and half conceal the Soul within' (*In Memoriam*), but my concern here is more with the predisposing mental images that each of us brings to our interpretation as a result of our previous experience of those words. It is these which guide us in our choice of the behaviours which flow from our instinctive reaction to the words and so affect the outcomes we each produce. It is these predisposing mental images that I wish to explore, particularly in the case of the word 'strategic'. However since, in my experience, its 'misinterpretation' arises from its very frequent association with the apparently more easily understood 'planning' I propose to begin my exploration there.

The Problem with 'Planning'

Writing in *Management Today* (the journal of the Institute of Management) in October 1994 David Morton reported: 'A recent study conducted by the

European Union on why it could not understand what the British were planning to do revealed that they were not planning to do anything.' He went on to describe the British as 'the world's great underachievers' at planning, concluding that we are, by nature, great improvisers – 'At improvisation we would win the World Cup.'

I cannot say with any certainty that these traits are, as Morton claims, both in-born and national, though my own experience suggests that the latter claim is accurate: most of the people with whom I have worked in this country do seem to find reacting to the immediate preferable as a form of activity to preparing for the future. This is not surprising. The immediate is known and most often demands a response; the future is often unknown, at least with any degree of precision, and dealing with it can usually be (with apparent safety) left until tomorrow. Particularly when you are very busy it is therefore easy to convince yourself that you must deal with today now, immediately or at least first, and that tomorrow can wait.

In no sphere of human activity is this – socially instinctive if not in-born – characteristic more prevalent than in the management of organisations. Managers are there (as perceived by most of us) to make decisions, help people achieve things and solve problems when they occur; in other words it is the manager's job to deal with the immediate. Managers are therefore, with very rare exceptions, by definition busy people. As the leading character in *The Disorganised Manager, part I – Damnation* (a training film produced by Video Arts) replies, when his personal guru (in this case St Peter played by John Cleese) accuses him of never planning anything, 'I haven't got time for planning.' However, useful as that anecdote is in illustrating what I believe to be one of the major contributory factors to the trait referred to in Morton's article, the kind of planning to which both manager and guru in the film are referring is not the kind to which Morton is alluding in his article. St Peter and his client are specifically dealing with the problems of the immediate – the need for personal organisation, in this instance to be provided in the form of short-term planning, to ensure that the total time available is used to best advantage.

This in turn reveals a further difficulty associated with our use and application of the word planning. When it is used it is very often related to the short or medium term in the sense of 'getting ready for' something which we know is going to happen and must therefore be prepared for. An analysis of time use with which I introduce school managers to a sense of their own current ordering of their priorities confirms the prevalence of this interpretation. It is based on a study made of over 3000 effective managers in different organisations. In order to promote useful analysis of their deployment of their time, the activities undertaken by these managers were all placed, with their agreement that this created an understandable and realistic model of their roles, in one of five broad categories:

- Planning
- Administering
- Leading and Guiding
- Controlling
- Representing

The average time spent on each of these categories of activity was then calculated with a view to supplying a reasonable guide for the activities of managers in similar positions (those with a number of other staff for whom they were responsible within a larger organisational system – such as heads of department in a school/college or headteachers within an old LEA).

When I introduce this analysis I always stress that the activities categorised under Planning refer to the long-term future of the organisation and not to activities which are directed to its achievement of current objectives. These latter are categorised as Administering, specifically in order to distinguish them from those more speculative activities a manager undertakes with an eye to future, as yet undefined, developments. Despite this, most of those meeting this analysis for the first time categorise activities such as 'Drawing up plans to cover Mrs X's absence on maternity leave next term', or (more understandably), 'Working on next year's timetable' as Planning. It is only when the recommended time allocation for each category is revealed and discussed, and they discover that planning in the sense used for this analysis accounts for only 'around 5 per cent' of a manager's time, that they realise how often their own interpretation of planning is linked to the concept of preparation and thus inevitably imports a sense of the short or medium term.

So the problem with planning appears to be twofold. We instinctively relate it predominately to activities concerned more with our need to be prepared for events we know are scheduled to happen in the short and medium term, than to consideration of longer-term possibilities. Perhaps linked to this tendency we also appear to eschew planning, at least in this long-term speculation sense, in favour of reacting, and therefore allocate very little or no time to it in our regular patterns of work. This leads me to consider, in similar vein, our instinctive understanding of the word strategic.

The Problem with 'Strategic'

As I write (mid-1996) the Teacher Training Agency (TTA) is in the process of creating the framework of the new National Professional Qualification for Headship (NPQH), the latest initiative of the present government in the field of education and the first time such a qualification has ever been sought in the United Kingdom. At the heart of the proposals towards the new qualification lies a newly defined 'standard' for school leadership. This sets out the core purpose of headship and five, associated, key areas for assessment and development through which headteachers achieve that purpose. Together these areas of the standard provide the conceptual framework around which the training and assessment for the new qualification will be developed.

Following consultation with representatives of the profession the TTA has decreed that the first of these five key areas – Strategic Planning and Development – will form the *core* of the new qualification. All candidates for the national qualification will have to demonstrate that they are competent in this area as their starting point towards the final award. Party to the early discussion of the government's proposal to establish such a qualification, I was present when it was decided not only to suggest this particular 'standard' approach to the framework for the NPQH but to recommend that it should include, as the first of the five key areas, one which focused specifically on a headteacher's capacity for leading the strategic development of her or his school. All those present, which included people with headship experience and two current deputy heads, agreed that the whole concept of strategy and its development was one about which schools still demonstrate less clear understanding than they reveal in most other aspects of their work. Those present also agreed that the work now carried out routinely in most schools under the heading of school development planning (though effective in its own terms) could rarely be described with any accuracy as strategic.

Consideration of strategy involves something more than the incremental moves forward that characterise the vast majority of school development plans – essential and effective as those are in the normal, day-to-day improvement of organisational effectiveness. Consideration of strategy has, I believe, to include something more of speculation about a range of possible but ill-defined futures than is easily promoted by a review which is firmly located in the desire simply to improve current practice. Calculation of the possible responses a school/college might make to the estimates of the future that such consideration makes possible, should also promote a reconsideration of the organisation's understanding of its own fundamental purpose and its confirmation, or amendment, of this in the light of its conclusions. Ultimately then the contemplation of strategy requires a willingness to suspend belief in present practice (however good that is) in the search for a possibly more meaningful future.

Incremental improvement processes in our experience tend to emphasise (very properly within their own terms of reference) the moves needed towards the achievement of already defined outcomes measured by the gains they can demonstrate against current levels of performance. Let me stress again that such processes are essential both to the actual, tangible improvement in a school's/college's provision for its pupils/students and, handled properly, to the continuing development of the staff. However, they are not, in my understanding of the word, strategic. And so to my understanding of strategic planning.

Strategic Planning

As must be becoming plain my concern in this book is to address specifically that kind of planning which does not relate to the short term or the incremental. I want to explore the various ways in which some people can and do set about preparing themselves and their organisations for different possible and as yet uncertain (if not unknown) futures. I am not talking here just about the currently fashionable idea of 'visioning' as a specific organisational process, though some element of vision as an important part of the strategic development of all organisations will feature later. What I wish to present are the best ideas I have met and worked with for placing some sort of pattern on the mass of different factors that are likely to affect an organisation in the longer term, so that more rational predictions can be arrived at and more reasoned choices made between apparent alternatives. The aim of this book therefore is to offer various ways of drawing up models or maps of your school/college so that you can project its possible future with more clarity: in short, and deliberately paraphrasing my own earlier comments, to help you construct a view of the future which has more of the character of the immediate, thus making the unknown more knowable.

So this book is about both strategy and planning, but planning as relating to the process by which school leaders may draw up usable maps of the future. This is because the essence or central focus of your attention, if you wish to take advantage of the book, must remain on the concept of strategy rather than on planning. As I have set out above, the problem with the word 'planning' is that it has the in-built implication of immediacy in its everyday usage. As a result its use tends to imply the existence of known problems or situations to which carefully applied forethought can provide definitive solutions or outcomes. It thus imports a unilinear and finite process, which tends not to embrace the ambiguous too easily nor to revisit naturally the assumptions from which it starts. This is revealed by the standard definitions to be found in dictionaries of the word 'plan' – 'a scheme for accomplishing a purpose' (*Chambers 20th Century Dictionary*). Thus, in the context of this book, the word 'map' more precisely conveys my meaning – a 'representation or epitome of the disposition or state of anything' (*Chambers* again). However, since in common use the phrase 'strategic mapping' has no normal currency I must adhere to the more usual phrase, 'strategic planning'. At the same time I must endeavour to ensure that we interpret it explicitly and consistently within the context of the future, with the clear intention of creating a representation of that future which can aid the further development of the school as an organisation.

Strategic Planning and School Development Planning – a Summary

In the not too distant past (say ten years ago) I would have asserted, from my experience of schools/colleges (including the one of which I was the head for 11 years), the following.

- The predominant, frequently overriding concern of school leaders was to ensure the consistent delivery of a good school experience for every pupil in a largely consistent and known world.
- The preoccupation of this concern with passing on a known and valued inheritance reduced long-term planning to a very subordinate position in the hierarchy of activities which most school leaders routinely undertook.
- Probably as a result of this, such long-term planning and thinking as did take place was most often conducted in the heads of one or two senior staff (most usually one, the head) and only put into writing (if at all) in the form of a policy statement or instruction to staff which, it was intended, would bring about changes designed to put right things that were not working well in the present systems.
- Such thinking/planning therefore almost always occurred as *a reaction* (even if an imaginative one) to present deficiencies.
- As a result, such planning owed little to the systematic consideration of the school's fundamental purposes and current ways of meeting them, and was best described in the words of the late Professor Eric Briault, in his conclusion to his research into the ways LEAs and schools coped with falling rolls in the 1970s and early 1980s: 'planned ad hocery'.

I would assert that this is no longer the case. The Technical and Vocational Educational Initiative, the continuing diminution in the role of local education authorities, the massive changes to schools which have flowed from a succession of legislation and, above all, the onset of local management and the virtually independent status conferred on the grant maintained (GM) sector have all contributed to the establishment and consolidation of school development planning as a routine part of school management. Its place in the normal range of activity for the school leader is now confirmed by its inclusion in the schedule of inspection set up by the Office for Standards in Education (Ofsted).

As a result in particular of the work of writers like Hargreaves and Hopkins (1991), most schools now produce excellent development plans. The best of these present the outcomes of a faithful and thorough audit of the school's present situation, a set of thoughtfully devised targets for its improvement (in the *immediate* future) and the relevant cost budgets needed to meet these. This is what is required of schools – principally by Ofsted and by the school's

own governors in pursuit of their responsibility for the good overall management of the school and of its finances in particular – and most schools now
meet this requirement very well. If this is so what more is needed by or would
benefit such schools/colleges and their leaders? My contention is that any
form of plan which has to meet these criteria must inevitably be limited to
representing primarily the *reactions* of its managers *to the present*.

In other words school development planning, though an essential tool
which brings many real benefits, has in fact reinforced the natural, predominant preoccupation of the manager with the management of the immediate.
And it has done so while enshrining it in an apparently futures-related
package. The result is that most school development plans are dominated by
descriptive, factual summaries of current positions and the perceived needs
to which these inevitably give rise. There is little evidence of serious analysis
of probable alternative futures and consequently even less of structured
exploration of the possible options for responding to these. School development is therefore almost invariably limited to the provision of 'more of the
same', even though more might well be better and the same may thus be an
improved version of what went before.

So that whether it is the needs of pupils, the expectations of their parents,
the demands of the world of work (and increasingly of the world of non-work,
at least in the sense of permanent paid employment), or teachers' own
perceptions of what is likely to be the most effective form of teaching and
learning which form the main focus of the plan, the outcomes are dogged
from the outset by the needs of the present and the expectations and anxieties
to which these give rise. Very, very rarely do current modes of development
planning promote speculation by schools about real alternatives to current
assumptions about the fundamentals which ultimately drive any organisation's thinking. In short, to borrow a military analogy, most current school
development planning is a tactical process, not a strategic one: it tends to
ensure that today's battle can be fought in better order (which is an essential
responsibility) but leaves tomorrow's war to sort itself out. My aim in this book
is to attempt to supply something towards that strategic capability for school
leaders, to explore a range of ideas and techniques which they can deploy to
achieve this more strategic overview of their schools. Which takes me, finally
in this opening chapter, to what for me is a sustaining thread in my thinking
about strategic planning – the link I make between strategic planning and
learning.

Strategic Planning and Learning

Like all other organisations at the close of the twentieth century, schools and
colleges are faced with almost uninterrupted change. Such is its current pace
and magnitude that it is no longer feasible to view each successive change as

a separate event which may be carefully prepared for in order to maximise the advantages it brings and minimise the inevitable upheaval that ensues. It is not even possible to regard the continuous stream of changes as a series of manageable events. The whole concept of 'the management of change' as a deliberate organisational strategy for which people can be prepared and trained is now redundant. Change is now a constant condition within which all organisations must learn to operate or risk significant if not total failure. Managing in times of continuing change has therefore become one of the central focuses of organisational leadership for heads and principals as much as for the leaders of any other type of organisation. Just about the only prediction which leaders can make with confidence about the conditions within which their organisations have to work is that tomorrow's will be substantially different from today's.

This undoubtedly adds significantly to the pressures which heads and principals feel as they go about their work. In my experience, however, the potential for that pressure to exhibit itself in the form of negative personal stress is far greater if the leader resists the notion put forward above concerning the need to conceive change as one of the main operational contexts of all management activity. Accepting therefore, for our purposes, that the notion *is* an accurate representation of today's organisational reality, heads and principals need to increase their coping skills in relation to this particular pressure.

If the inevitable centrality of change is the bad news for school/college leaders the good news is (or can be) that they are better placed to handle the pressure it brings than leaders in many other kinds of organisation. Schools and colleges are organisations whose core business is learning, and it is my contention that the process of continual adaptation to changing circumstance which is required in order to manage effectively in times of continuing change is very akin to learning, or at least to learning in the experiential sense.

It was one of the main researchers (Kolb, 1984) into the ways that we all learn from our experience who described learning as a 'continuous, holistic process of adaptation'. From this description, and from my own work in the field of experiential learning (with adult learners on training courses) comes my conviction that the types of strategic planning process which are most likely to be effective are those which most closely follow the patterns which can be discerned from successful learning experiences. My interpretation of strategic planning itself is thus strongly influenced by my understanding of the learning process (and especially by the models of effective experiential learning which I have seen used successfully).

Learning therefore provides the background to my selection of the approaches to strategic planning in the chapters following. In fact the whole book might well be fancifully (though not necessarily inaccurately) represented as a personal journey of exploration of 'the Islands of Strategic Planning through the Sea of Learning'. I will return briefly to that theme in my closing chapter. For now I leave it with you in the hope that something of my specific conviction may help you follow my interpretation of strategic planning and, much more importantly, perhaps lead you successfully to apply one or more of the approaches to it which I suggest.

2

Systems Analysis: The Classic Approach to Strategic Planning

Introduction to the Different Approaches

This and the following chapters in effect tell and retell the 'story' of strategic planning from the standpoint of different possible observers. Each version provides an alternative method or approach through which an attempt can be made to capture (and learn from) some picture of the possible futures facing any school/college for the purpose of better developing the present to meet the challenges those futures may pose.

I provide several alternative approaches because, while I am convinced that it is essential for every school and college to try to create a map of its possible future, I do not believe there is one perfect method of doing this which will appeal to, and therefore be effective for, everyone. Just as each of us has our own preferred style of learning from our experience so schools and colleges – in the form of the teams of people who formulate their policies and thus determine the directions they will follow – develop preferred ways of thinking about their present state and future development. Any one of the methods described (in some cases even a part of a method) can add to the store of thinking capability of a school or college. Thus employing any *one* of these approaches will increase a school's ability to learn more about its possible futures from its current practice. Understanding each of them and then making a conscious choice which to deploy in one's own situation is in itself a first step towards this improved learning capacity. On the other hand...

...A Health Warning

Remember that too close a reliance on other people's panaceas is bad for you! Utilising any one of the approaches too rigidly or slavishly can have the countervailing effect of constraining an organisation's ultimate potential for development. None are panaceas or absolute solutions. In particular, schools and colleges are complex forms of organisation. Both the external and internal contexts in which they work are forever shifting and their response to these, if it is to succeed, has to be planned consciously to reflect the innate ambiguity which this complexity brings.

I can promise that I and others have effectively used, at different times and to suit different situations, each of the approaches presented in this book. What I am cautioning here is that as well as making your own choice of which approach appears to you to suit your needs best, you must apply your chosen approach with imagination as well as with respect for the recommended methodology. Too literal or slavish an attempt to apply your chosen method will inevitably diminish its effectiveness, and possibly on some occasions destroy it. The approaches recommended here are not a series of repair manuals any more than your school/college is a car. They are more akin, as implied above, to maps and in particular to road maps: they can help you plan your journey but by themselves they cannot choose the best route for your particular purpose. Nevertheless, while applying your chosen approach with imagination, it is necessary to respect its recommended methodology. This is not because this represents an ideal or perfect state, but because failure to do so will lead inevitably to you substituting your existing view of the world of your school/college for the alternative perspective the approach seeks to promote. Simply amending the recommended approach without thought to fit your current situation will limit if not destroy its potential as a strategic tool: in particular it will not lead you to the fundamental questions that need to be asked about your present purposes and forms of organisation if the future is to be faced with renewed clarity. So apply it imaginatively rather than slavishly but trust it; your existing patterns of thinking will easily superimpose themselves if trust is absent.

The Systems Analysis Approach

In no case is the danger referred to above more likely to occur than in the first approach which is set out in the remainder of this chapter and the next. The classic approach to strategic planning, and the one beloved by most corporate planners in large business organisations everywhere for the last 50 years or so, is the one rooted in the methodology known as *Systems Analysis*. As the name suggests this approach views the whole issue of organisational growth from the perspective of a series of interrelated, sometimes interlocking, sometimes overlapping, systems, the analysis of which will provide a complete map or diagrammatic representation of the organisation, its present state and range of possible futures.

Preceding the part of the process which is itself described as Systems Analysis is a preliminary stage described by practitioners as Strategic Positioning. The overall Systems Analysis approach therefore has two parts.

1. *Strategic Positioning* – a review of the organisation's current place in its own, external and internal, working contexts.
2. *Systems Analysis* – a step-by-step examination of the organisation's objectives and the various processes by which it currently seeks to achieve these.

Since both parts are subdivisions of the whole they inevitably interact; decisions, guesstimates or assumptions made in one part clearly affect another. Nevertheless it is useful to present the key elements which make up each part separately first. These are listed in Figures 2.1 and 2.2. The terminology used in both of these lists is exactly as I first met it at the hands of a management development director of a major British company in 1982. The 'translation' into equivalent educational terminology follows. However, since this is a model derived initially from the world of business it seems best to present it first in its original terminology. In that way if it loses anything in translation readers may form their own judgement of that loss and react accordingly.

Strategic Positioning

Made up of:

1. Markets
2. Business environment/competition
3. Products
4. Present objectives: targets and performance criteria, profit, growth and market share
5. Current resource deployment
6. Forecast of the future

Figure 2.1 *Key elements of Strategic Positioning*

Systems Analysis

1. Objectives to be achieved
2. Possible alternative ways of reaching these objectives
3. Cost and resources required to implement each objective by the chosen route – ie action plans
5. Contingency plans and reviews
6. A model to show the interdependence of objectives, systems, environment and resources

---

Figure 2.2 *Key elements of Systems Analysis*

Here now is my transcription of the terminology comprising the various elements of these two parts of the strategic planners' systems analysis approach. At this stage I have deliberately not limited myself to single-word or phrase alternatives to the original: in each case I have added my own explanation of what I think each element may be best taken to refer to in the world of schools and colleges. Once again readers are encouraged to refer my interpretation to the originals, make their own judgement of the accuracy of my perceptions and be prepared to substitute their own if mine are found wanting.

Strategic Positioning

1. Markets

What are the groups of potential pupils (parents?) and other users which the school is seeking to serve?
   Elements to be considered in responding to this question are as follows:

● geographical catchment areas (natural and extended);
● particular categories of pupil (eg physically handicapped, musically gifted);
● other kinds of learners (eg adults in day community schools);
● other potential users of the school's facilities (eg local business/community groups).

2. Business environment/competition

What are the prevailing external conditions within which all schools/colleges are having to operate – now and in the immediate, clearly discernible, future?
   Elements to be considered:

● national and local legislation and policies (eg National Curriculum, Ofsted, Further Education Funding Council (FEFC));
● economic situation (national and local);
● local demographic factors;
● other local schools/colleges;
● fashion (ie current social/educational vogues and prejudices).

3. Products

What is it that the school/college aims to deliver to its principal clients/users? A school's principal products are the range of high quality learning opportunities it provides – both within the formal, taught curriculum and alongside/around it – as a result of the work of its teaching and non-teaching staff.

However, the resources brought together to enable these basic products to be provided allow schools/colleges (where they wish to do so) to provide many other kinds of service to their chosen communities, eg learning and activity spaces for external groups.

Elements to be considered are as follows:

- Particular specialisms offered by the school (eg sporting prowess, artistic challenge).
- The particular emphasis of the basic school provision (eg selective teaching providing for the most or least able, or an explicit commitment to providing skills of lifelong learning).
- Specific advantages provided by the school's natural resources (eg geographical location, centre of historical significance).
- Any distinctive staffing qualities/abilities available to pupils/students.
- Resources – of space, equipment, time or staff expertise – which the school/college decides to make available to other users.

Note: Pupils/students are *not* products. I believe that anyone in education who indulges in this prime fallacy, which appeared to gain considerable credence some years ago, is in the wrong business. It should be inconceivable for anyone working with young people to view them as inanimate raw material to be moulded or made into some form of artefact.

4. Present objectives: targets and performance criteria, growth, market share – and profit

What is the school/college *specifically aiming to achieve* and what is the *added value*, for the benefit of pupils/students/other chosen users, which that will provide?

Elements to be considered include the following.

- What specific, measurable things are we trying to achieve and how will we know if/when we have achieved them (a reduction in the overall rates of non-attendance or an increase in the proportion of local parents making this school their first choice, for instance)?
- What do *we* mean in this school by profit? Are we waiting to be told about 'value added' or do we want to set our own measures of input and output? (For example, a secondary school which measured the reading ages of all its pupils at entry (Year 7), set individual targets for each one to reach by the middle of Year 9 when they were retested, and so could demonstrate to parents the 'profit' shown by the school in that one crucial, core-skill area.)

- What does this school reckon is its potential for growth? Is this just calculated in numbers of pupils? If so has the school established its own figures for its optimum size – taking into account the size of the campus, its current buildings, its sense of the number (of pupils) at which a school/college begins to lose its sense of cohesion as a community?
- If it is not concerned with numbers how can the school grow in terms of its facilities and/or the range of educational opportunities it offers to its pupils/students?
- Has the school established for itself what share of the total potential 'market' (of available pupils, other learners/users) it wants to attract? If it has set itself an increase in its current share of the market has it considered the effect of this on other local providers? What are the potential gains/ losses in ignoring that sense in which individual schools are part of larger local communities? Too ready, uncritical acquiescence to the inevitability of competition leads to the potential diminution of the school's ability to provide a sound model for its pupils/students in a key aspect of citizenship.

Note: This is one of the most difficult aspects of the world of business to translate effectively into the world of schools and colleges. To avoid too much interruption at this point of the pattern of thinking espoused by this approach there is a detailed note of my own response to this difficulty at the end of the chapter.

5. Current resource deployment

How are the current resources available to the school used?
    Elements to be considered:

- Finance available: routine and non-routine sources.
- Buildings and equipment (their maintenance in good order to contribute to a positive environment for learning).
- Staff – the separate and collective expertise of non-teaching and teaching staff – is the current balance as good as it could be? Would an experienced business manager provide more of what this large secondary school/ college needs rather than a second (or third) deputy? Have we really calculated the immense value – to the pupils' overall learning experience – provided by a good school office in a primary school? Are we rewarding the staff concerned properly?
- Curriculum systems – especially the timetable. (Does it really represent the most effective distribution of pupil time or is it designed largely as a result of staff's traditional expectations? What are its best features? What constraints does it impose?)
- Management systems – are these deployed specifically so as to *enable* the work of the staff or are they more an expression of professional status?

What are the criteria by which we in our school arrive at this distinction? Who sets these criteria? Have they ever been explicitly considered?

6. Forecasts of the future

What sort of picture of the future can we (a) fairly confidently predict in the short to medium term (the next three to five years) and (b) envision for the longer term (ten years plus)?

The elements to be considered here are all contained under one or more of the previous five headings in this review. However crucial ones, using the shorthand of the original model in Figure 2.1, are as follows:

- Market – are any changes likely to be forced on the school or desirable for it to seek?
- Business environment/competition – accurately predicting legislative/ political/social change (the business environment of education) in detail is impossible, but ignoring obvious trends and possibilities is foolhardy. What about competitors? And what new ranges of alternative educational provision may developing technologies provide?
- Products and present objectives – how 'future proofed' is the present offering the school makes? Are the criteria by which it judges its current work future oriented at all or entirely dependent on traditional practice?
- How much of this traditional practice seems to be needed for the future? Check market share intentions against the picture of possible future markets.

'SWOT it'

Yes, you've got it! What has been described in the preceding pages under the heading 'Strategic Positioning' is one specific form of the now familiar SWOT (**S**trengths, **W**eaknesses, **O**pportunities, and **T**hreats) analysis. This is often trotted out as *the* essential panacea for all those who aspire to strategically plan anything. There is no doubt that it is a very memorable acronym, particularly – with its connotations of hard study – for teachers.

I have left mention of it until now simply because when I first met this particular systems analysis approach to strategic planning I found that the explicit consideration of each of the separate aspects of the school's strategic position provided me with the essential framework for my own SWOT analysis. Without it I was left to flounder in a much more subjective form of assessment of the school's strengths and weaknesses, which was dependent very largely upon my own current sense of well-being or malaise about the school; and I found 'opportunities' and 'threats' almost impossible triggers to which to respond.

However, once I applied **S**, **W**, **O** and **T** in turn to each of the elements of the strategic positioning review of the school, I began to put some real flesh on the bones of my analysis. In many cases the same factors emerged under more than one heading. Some seemed to provide both opportunity *and* threat. And this repetition and apparent bifocalism proved to be a real advantage rather than a problem. For one thing they stopped me trying to make my review too detailed: the frequent reoccurrence of some factors seemed to force me back to the broad-brush picture which was essential if I was to distil the key messages for the school's future development. Conversely they helped me identify some of the key features which we would need to take into account if we were going to move the school forward strategically.

This latter effect, however, also depended to a great extent upon the impact on my sense of the strategic positioning of the school which came from the concurrent consideration of the other part of the process – the Systems Analysis. So let me now turn to my transposition of that part of the process (set out in Figure 2.2 on page 13) into the working terminology of schools and colleges. This can be much more easily achieved than was the case with the Strategic Position, because the terms used are themselves more familiar now to schools and colleges.

In the case of the first element of the Systems Analysis there is considerable overlap with elements of the review of the Strategic Position. Nevertheless, there is a difference between them which it is important to establish before moving on. Broadly, the Strategic Position reviews the *current state* of the school within its external and internal contexts. The consideration of the external contexts inevitably has to include a view of possible changes which may occur in the future.

The Systems Analysis *looks entirely to the future*. It picks up the internal contexts (revealed by the Strategic Position) and, guided by the assumptions about the future which can be derived from the strategic positioning review, defines the school's possible range of responses.

In short, Strategic Positioning helps us see where we are now as a school. Systems Analysis then enables us to plot possible courses to follow in the future.

Systems Analysis

1. *Objectives to be achieved*

Consideration of this aspect obviously starts from a rerun of the fourth element of the Strategic Position review. The difference here is that, by the time it reaches this point in the process, any school should be aiming to make a positive selection of those objectives it believes it should pursue in the future. The range of options open for selection will be defined by the school's current purposes as reviewed against the assumptions and guidelines drawn from the review of the school's Strategic Positioning and its forecasts about the future.

As this is a strategic exercise these objectives should be concerned with establishing the broad pattern of the school's development – its principal targets. These in turn will be strongly influenced and in some cases determined by other aspects of the strategic review, particularly those arising from a study of markets/competition/product (ie the school's/college's purpose: precisely what business do we want this school to be in within the broad field of schooling/education?). There should not therefore be too many of these, both because a large number will be impossible to manage and deliver and because the emergence of a very large number will indicate that the labelling of these targets has slipped from the strategic to the tactical level.

Finally it is necessary to summarise the total list of objectives selected within a short, overall statement of purpose. This reveals two things: the degree of congruence between the various objectives and their total coherence in relation to the school's central focus on what it is trying to achieve.

2. Alternative ways of reaching these objectives

This element speaks for itself. However, it is worth stressing that to maintain the *strategic* view of the school which this approach promotes it is essential that the ways and means, in relation to each selected objective in turn, are considered *after* that objective has been firmly placed within the school's overall development strategy. If ways are considered at the same time as purposes there is an inevitable tendency to shy away from some of the most strategic choices just because the means of achieving them do not spring easily to mind. The inevitable consequence of this is that the school/college simply produces 'more of the same' for the future, regardless of the quality of its review of its strategic position and the messages about possible futures which this revealed.

Furthermore it is important to consider *more than one* possible way of reaching an objective. This has benefits: it immediately challenges any tendency towards the 'that's impossible' reaction noted above, and each successive alternative has the effect of offering a critical yardstick against which to measure its predecessor – and vice versa. The net result is often to arrive at the most effective choice of the way ahead by an amalgam of more than one of the alternatives considered.

3. Cost and resources required to implement each chosen objective: action plans

It is almost inevitable that first-level estimates of the costs of each alternative considered at point 2 above formed part of that consideration. It is probable that such estimates will be one of the criteria used for determining the preferred alternative.

However, it is now important to go one step further and prepare an outline action plan (with dates) for each selected alternative. This in turn promotes a second-level, more detailed (though still 'broad-brush') calculation of all the resources required. In particular it is vital at this stage to specify where the *staff time* required to see through the implementation is to come from; only then can the total effect of the proposed strategies on the school as a whole be calculated. Without this calculation even the most carefully selected strategies will have a very good chance of failing to achieve what they are intended to achieve.

A recent example of this occurred in a school which arrived at a most visionary but achievable view of its own future as a result of a process which involved a very large proportion of its staff (both teaching and non-teaching) and representatives of other key stakeholders such as parents and governors. One key aspect of the plan which the school produced to implement its vision depended upon a continuance of this key principal of staff involvement at every level of the organisation alongside a conscious move towards a different model of leadership for the school. In pursuance of these aims groups were established to work on each of the objectives and the management of the school set about empowering many others to take on the kind of decision-making responsibility which had formerly rested only in the hands of the traditional senior team. The good news is that these intentions are still in place. However, failure to calculate the key aspect of staff time involved has put a significant brake on progress. The school's new team leaders require (and quite properly want to receive) some form of structured introduction to and preparation/training for their changed roles, not least lest they fall into the obvious trap of simply replacing a traditional top-down senior management system with a top-down version of middle management. The failure to calculate the total effect of the modes of implementation the school is seeking to follow is that there is currently no time left for this training to take place. Everyone involved is already fully committed as a member, in almost every case, of more than one of the groups working on the other objectives: and this, as always in school, on top of a continuing full teaching and administrative load.

That anecdote should not be read as indicating the impossibility of *ever* moving a school forward strategically by this means. The school itself admits that it could have foreseen this difficulty and planned for it. They have done so now by delaying some other aspects of the implementation process in order to create time/space for the necessary training.

5. Contingency plans and reviews

One of my other initial key insights was the assumption the planner took that one or more of the strategies for implementation was bound to fail, or at least require significant amendment in the light of new factors which are revealed as implementation progresses. To prepare for this eventuality it is necessary, from the outset, to identify, at a broad level, a wholly different alternative view of each objective. This is the 'what if' scenario or contingency plan referred to here.

It is not necessary to have a detailed contingency plan to parallel the action plan. Rather what is called for is a conscious focusing on any key stage where the implementation is clearly dependent on factors outside the direct control of the school. Wherever such a stage is identified it is important to ask 'What do we do if the worst happens?' Sometimes the answer will be 'Well, we just won't proceed with that but the rest of our strategy can still be maintained.' At other times the failure to implement one key strategy will have an unavoidable impact on others. One obvious example is the loss of expected funding for building development on which a new, larger, intake of students has been based. Of course it is impractical to attempt to second-guess every possible eventuality; what is required instead is a systematic review of each objective and the total strategy promoted by the analysis to see where the most likely and the most damaging contingencies might occur.

Finally, to cope with those which do occur and to continue a vigilant watch on the possible range of 'what if' scenarios, the school needs to include in every action plan a routine system of review which can track the various contingencies and convert than into revised action plans as and when necessary.

6. A model to show the interdependence of objectives, systems, environment and resources

The value of such a model is that it presents a straightforward picture of the whole process described in both the review of strategic position and the Systems Analysis procedure. Each constituent part of the picture then becomes a locus for the collection of information by the school towards its strategic plan: what the professional planners call 'strategic databases'.

The model to which I was introduced when I first met this approach is given at Figure 2.3. I hope that, relating it to the various discrete elements of the process which have gone before, it is at least visually self-explanatory. However, there is one box on the model which has been mentioned only obliquely so far – that labelled Assumptions and Guidelines. You will see that the information in this particular database is derived from both the Future Forecasts and the school's Statement of Purpose/Objectives/Individual Strategies. You will also note that the data arising *from* the Assumptions and Guidelines base contributes *to* the school's/college's delineation of its core purpose/objectives. In this latter case the relationship between these two databases is more quintessentially symbiotic than at any of the other points on the model where this quality is indicated by the double-arrowed lines.

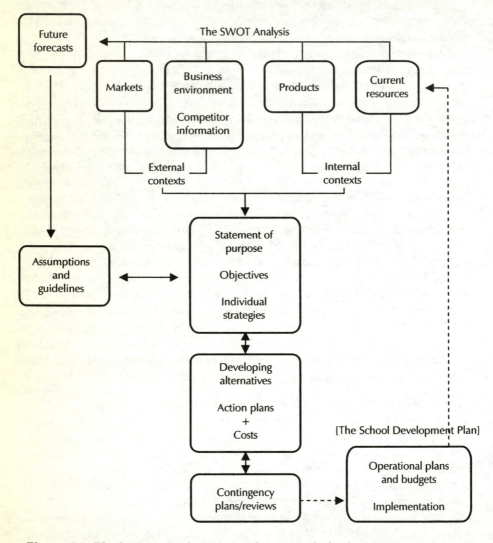

Figure 2.3 *The Systems Analysis approach – strategic databases*

The importance of this extra database lies in the nature and quality of the link it can provide between the Strategic Positioning and Systems Analysis parts of this process. Without a careful analysis of the *assumptions* we use in interpreting the information drawn from the other databases, and an examination of the *guidelines* these imply for our decisions about how to proceed as a result of these assumptions, a vital link in our strategic thinking remains unchecked. There is great danger in relying on unchecked assumptions. As the well-known saying goes: In working with others in an organisation there is always a risk that anything we ASSUME may make an ASS out of U and ME.

Nowhere is that risk greater than if we fail to check the assumptions on which we base our conclusions about the range of strategies by which we propose to face the future. It is essential that we seek to examine the prejudices and preconceptions which make us arrive at those conclusions.

Almost for this reason alone the next chapter provides an exercise for you to trial the Systems Analysis approach in general and this part – assumptions and guidelines – in particular. It is in the form of a case study through which you can decide which are the crucial facts of a situation, reveal the assumptions to which these appear to give rise and distil the guidelines or goals towards which they point. The exercise may be conducted on your own or with a group of colleagues. It illustrates the key aspect of the Systems Analysis approach – the distillation of the elements most directly bearing upon strategic decision-making from the mass of factors involved in any overall review of the organisation. The case study is deliberately set in business rather than in educational contexts. This is to provoke the distancing effect which helps focus attention on the key aspects of the analysis without involving readers in too subjective an interpretation of the factors which make up the situation.

If you feel it would be helpful to test your own understanding of the Systems Analysis approach now please go straight to the case study exercise. It is followed by a commentary. This contains some further 'health warnings' about applying the model shown in Figure 2.3 in the real-life world of a school or college. It also includes positive recommendations regarding its use, which can enhance the quality of the sense of strategic purchase which this whole approach is designed to provide. Read this commentary before tackling the exercise if you prefer, though it is probably advisable to 'have a go' at *using* the Systems Analysis approach through this case study situation before considering these further tips concerning its deployment in the real world.

The Notion of 'Profit' in Educational Organisations

Finally here is the note on profit which I promised earlier.

I do not believe it is in any way satisfactory, in educational organisations, simply to reiterate platitudes such as 'we live in a competitive world' or 'education has to exist in a free market'. Such assertions in themselves deny much of the value-driven basis of education which is essential for the delivery of effective learning opportunities to young people. That is a bad enough effect but one which can be challenged by the determination of teachers who instinctively resist the potentially negative import of such limitations on their work with pupils. However, in the context of strategic development, as bad an effect is that which such simplistic interpretation can have on the staff in schools and colleges in making them instinctively resist the very important message which this aspect of the strategic review of their position *should* carry for them: that is the need for all organisations to make clear to themselves precisely what it is they are trying to achieve. In my experience a very large proportion of educational organisations are still driven by the sense of what they have to *do*, far more than by a clear perception of what they are there to *achieve*.

At one level a preoccupation with 'doing' is both relevant and proper: it focuses attention sharply on the current generation of pupils/students and their immediate needs. In the 1960s and 1970s I certainly witnessed many schools who were so concerned with preparing for a future social and educational tomorrow that they left themselves very little time and even less energy for today's pupils. One glaring example of this was a school where the drive towards the future was so powerful that virtually all teaching staff were meeting in a series of differently constituted groups (of subject departments, pastoral teams and special curriculum development working parties) after school on three days in every full week of the term. On the fourth evening in the week those staff with additional responsibilities (the head, deputies, pastoral team leaders, working party chairs and heads of departments) met together as a policy steering group, and once a month the fourth evening was used for either a full staff meeting (everyone expected) chaired by the head/deputy or an open staff forum (convened and led by the chair of common room committee with voluntary attendance). As a result, with the honourable exception of the PE department and the termly drama productions, after-school activities had virtually (and inevitably) ceased, not to mention the lost opportunities for *ad hoc* conversations with pupils after school which otherwise characterised the best schools I came across then (and still come across now). That school, whose staff were in their minds doing everything they did for the ultimate benefit of the pupils (of tomorrow), had somewhat lost sight of what it was there to achieve – a vibrant and fulfilling learning experience for the pupils of today. Most staff had little or no time (or energy) for anything outside their routine teaching duties and the demands of the meetings they attended.

So there is a need for schools to focus clear attention and significant energy on today's pupils: every one of them has only one trip through the tunnel of scholastic experience. This note is not designed to undermine a school's/ college's proper concern for that part of its responsibility. However, if this proper concern for today becomes the obsessive, dominant (only?) focus of a school it also inevitably moulds the school community into modes of behaviour which are almost entirely concerned with doing what needs doing. This in turn makes it more likely that the school will lose sight of the overall purposes which it set out to pursue. Continued over even a moderate length of time this focus on 'busy work' can lead to a narrowing of experience, a predominant concern with survival and a consequent lowering of expectation to the lowest of common denominators.

Focusing attention consciously on what the school/college is striving to *achieve* (rather than on what it is doing) acts as a powerful antidote to the tendency noted above. Schools are busy places and today's pupils/students are properly their first concern. But I believe that concern can only be adequately fulfilled if what we are doing is regularly checked against the template of what it is we, as teachers, are trying to achieve. If we only concentrate on what we have to do then, within the natural boundaries of moral and professional behaviour, whatever actions we choose to pursue are by definition as justifiable and as likely to be effective as any other. Only by asking how those chosen courses of action contribute (for the pupils) to what we are striving to achieve (for the pupils) can we discriminate effectively between the various options and prioritise our time, energy and resources appropriately.

At the whole school level – the level which determines the broad patterns of school activity and thereby sets the conditions which establish and maintain the school's culture – it is our continual readiness to check our objectives, to seek to define our own sense of 'profit' in what we are doing, that is most likely to provide the essential antidote for busy work. So I make no apologies for asserting that schools/colleges, and in particular their managers and governors, should address the question of 'profit': they are there to make a 'profit' for their pupils/students by ensuring that each of them gains demonstrable benefit from their time in the school.

3

Applying the Systems Analysis Approach

This chapter consists of a case study exercise followed by some further tips on the effective use of Systems Analysis.

The Case Study

Premium Goods Ltd

PGL is a family-run but publicly owned producer of premium electronic consumer products. Although the product line is limited the company has a reputation for high quality and the employees are proud to work for it.

Unlike many companies in the industry, the average tenure of PGL's 4000 employees is over 20 years, and many employees spend their entire career there. Because the company is located in a small town and has always provided stable employment many children follow their parents into the company; there are third-generation employees throughout PGL. Most employees are members of a small union, which until recently has had a fairly cooperative, family-like relationship with the company management.

PGL also provides a great social outlet for employees. The company owns a residential training centre based on an old country house estate. This is used frequently for company celebrations, employee recognition events and other gatherings. It includes a leisure complex and swimming pool which is open to all the employees and their families.

Until five years ago the company held over 50 per cent of the market share for its product line and was very profitable, with 1990 net sales and operating revenues of £159 million producing a profit of £7.8 million. Its share has since eroded to 27 per cent due to an influx of foreign competition and other UK companies using more modern, cost-effective technologies. The company anticipates an operating loss of £8 million this year and its stock is currently the lowest it has ever been. Suggestions of possible layoffs have received strong negative reactions from employees, as well as directly from the union, which has talked about affiliating with a larger union for the first time.

At the insistence of the non-executive directors the board hired a consulting firm to review the company, its management structure and market environment. Following an intensive three-month study the consulting firm issued a report focusing on several key issues.

One of the report's main findings was that the product remains the best-regarded name in the category, but the majority of consumers think it is too highly priced. The major operational findings are given below.

1. Operating costs have skyrocketed, partly in response to union demands for higher wages and salaries in the light of the company's successful sales/profit records some years ago.
2. The capital equipment is fully depreciated but outdated. Updating and maintenance of obsolete equipment is the largest item of expenditure after wages and it is increasing.
3. The sales force is not experienced in competing on a cost-benefit basis with cheaper imports. It has always relied on the reputation of the company's products and its long-standing name in the electronic goods market.

The company is playing a losing game of catch-up by sticking to its premium quality, higher cost strategy.

The report concluded that PGL has not responded to changing market demands and technology, and suggests that new blood be brought in to bring the company back to life and implement new strategies. Basically, it is the consulting firm's opinion that the company is too concerned with the welfare and security of its employees, which is a short-term goal, at the expense of its own longer-term viability, a conclusion which has split the board.

In a surprise move, however, the board acted on the report's recommendations, gave the founder's son (who was Chairman) early retirement, hired a new MD under a very lucrative performance-based contract and put in a non-executive chairman. The new MD is young, forceful and has a string of company revival successes behind him at the age of 44. He is very aggressive and tough minded, focusing on bottom-line results and, although he is new to the product line, he is a brilliant administrator and strategic thinker.

The first thing he did was to lure you away from PGL's major competitor with a good starting salary and the opportunity for bonuses in the form of shares in PGL. He gave you the post of Director of Strategic Development. Your interest in the opportunity, apart from increased responsibility and salary, lies in helping turn around a basically fine company, something you have never done before. After 30 days on the job, he calls you into his office and says:

I want you to give me your view as to what the problem is and tell me what strategies you think we should work on. What specifically do you believe we should do? I'm an action-oriented person, but I want to do this right. I would like your views as soon as possible.

Using the Case Study to Cement your Understanding of the Systems Analysis Approach: Guidelines for the Exercise

Step 1

Having read the case study, and using the model in Figure 2.3 as a guide, *identify the facts* which reveal the strategic position of the company by highlighting or underlining and labelling (see below) each of them in the text above.

Labelling

As you identify each fact indicate its specific import as a contributory factor in terms of the company's markets (M), its business environment (E) , its products (P) or current use of its resources (R). Identify which of them represents a strength (S), a weakness (W), an opportunity (O) or a threat (T) for the company.

This can be done either directly on the text of the case study as suggested above or (my preference) on a sheet of A3 paper with a rough outline of the model from Figure 2.3 reproduced on it. A blank version of Figure 2.3 is attached at the end of this chapter for you to photocopy and enlarge if you wish.

Step 2

You have no detailed information about the actual conditions of trading which the company may face in the future, but make whatever *forecast* about the company's future from the information you have distilled from the case study that you can.

Step 3

Now *identify the assumptions* underlying your analysis in Step 1 and whatever forecast you have made in Step 2. These are the fundamentals – the beliefs, hunches, values – upon which your strategy will be based. They arise from your perceptions of the present situation and the messages you draw from them about the best possible response the company can make to secure its likely future. This is a critical step.

Step 4

Having checked your underlying assumptions *set out each of the issues/problems* which you believe the company must address.

Step 5

Now *define the goals* (the things the company must achieve to resolve the issues/problems it faces) and divide these into short-term (objectives) and longer-term (core purpose) categories.

Step 6

Describe (briefly) *the action(s)* you recommend should be taken now.

Note: A test run of this Systems Analysis model is incomplete if it does not include an action step (Step 5, above). However, do not attempt to carry this step too far. You are not in possession of enough detailed information about the company's finances, staffing situation, stocks, manufacturing procedures etc to go very far down this route and, for our purpose here (of trialling the underlying fundamentals which it is necessary to review if we are to capture the strategic position of an organisation successfully) it is only necessary to establish the essential connection to action which completes the Systems Analysis.

Some Further Tips on the Application of this Approach

It is one thing to describe the approach set out in the previous chapter. It does not seem to me sufficient to leave it at that and expect anyone, on the basis of that description alone, to be able to make immediate, effective use of it. Here are several further tips which I believe are helpful in making the approach more accessible in practical terms.

Time

Time is the first and most consistent worry of all school/college managers. I would be very surprised if many readers who have read this far aren't by now saying to themselves (at best!) something like, 'Yes: all very interesting but no way have I/we got the *time* to make use of that.' That is the inevitable price I (and you) must pay for the amount of detail in which I felt it was necessary to set out this first approach to strategic development. Partly as a way of attempting to secure your conviction (alongside my own) about a mode of analysis so clearly established in the world of business, and partly to try to give you the benefit of my own way of interpreting the different elements of the approach in order to make use of it, I believe the amount of exposition which I have provided was necessary.

Nevertheless, complex and time consuming as that amount of description may have made it seem, the approach does not have to be applied in a time-consuming way to be useful. When I first met it I was presented with the model (in the form of Figures 2.1 and 2.2) by way of an overhead. I was then invited to perform a rapid analysis of the school (of which I was at that time the head) on the basis of the model and was given about ten minutes' worth of verbal explanation of each of the databases. The speaker gave us about 15 minutes to complete this initial analysis before we began to discuss it. Although at that stage I had nothing written in some of the boxes, eg Products, a further ten minutes or so of discussion on these enabled me to at least make a start in all of them and, more importantly, sent me back to school sufficiently equipped to carry out a fuller version of the analysis later that week. In the event I did not even then spend more than a further hour or so on it before I began to *feel* the benefits it provided in two ways.

Even used in this relatively superficial but certainly time-efficient way it made me bring crucial aspects of my school sharply into focus, where before I had either omitted consideration of them altogether or left them on the periphery of my thinking. This was usually either because they seemed to me to lie entirely outside my ken (eg the Business environment was one I found I'd almost consciously ignored until then) or because they did not seem susceptible to influence by me whatever I did, such as the issue of Markets. (This *was* the early 1970s, before such horrendous concepts had burst so forcibly on the educational scene!)

On top of this, an important effect of the model overall was to provide a coherent framework within which to contemplate all these factors at once, and so begin to discern the ways in which they interacted with each other and how consciously addressing some of them was in itself almost sufficient to bring out their influence on others. Thus in the case of my partly ignored area of the marketplace I was made aware that at least acquiring more information about that aspect of the school would be helpful to myself and the staff in deciding where to place some of our priorities in the coming years: I didn't have either to *believe* in marketing or know very much about the concept of the marketplace to gain this much advantage. At the time the school had a falling roll in an urban setting where there was (because of a decline in the local birth rate which had already far outstripped national trends) something of the order of 1000 pupils per age group of secondary age against an estimated capacity across the town at large of nearer 1500 pupils per age group. We (I) had therefore assumed there was nothing we could (or should) do about this situation. Just raising the question of the marketplace to the level of an *unavoidable* influence on the contexts within which the school had to operate (as the model did for me) made us seek more information about our specific share of the overall market. This revealed some very interesting reasons about why parents who could have chosen to send their pupils did not do so. One of these in particular we felt was an issue we could and should do something about. We did, and our share of the market improved slightly, but just as importantly we learned something about ourselves and the way we chose to work with pupils at that time which had far-reaching effects outside the specific area of change we chose to make.

I am conscious that the weakness of that anecdote may well lie in the fact that it focuses on the marketplace, which is now automatically such a central concern of most schools in the wake of successive governments' explicit espousal of a free market for education (as well as for water, widgets and the general well-being of society). It is probably also true that schools now have many more sophisticated tools of analysis, which they are accustomed to using, than we had in the 1970s. My main purpose in setting the anecdote before you is to demonstrate the potential of this approach as a relatively speedy and summary form of usable analysis rather than the time-consuming monster about which I may have left you in despair at the end of the last chapter.

Using the systems analysis model to conduct a whole-organisation review of strategy

Although I said that I found the approach of almost instant help to my own thinking it clearly can be used much more fully. In particular it provides a template for a whole-school process of strategic review and development which differs in some important respects from other, better-known examples.

The best known of these are probably either the Department for Education and Employment's (DfEE) own 'School Development Planning' model pioneered by Hargreaves and Hopkins (1991) and the earlier Guidelines for the Review and Institutional Development of Schools (GRIDS) system set up from the School of Education at Bristol. I have already commented that, good as the Hargreaves and Hopkins approach is as a routine for school planning, for me it lacks the essentially deeper probing which a review system aimed at developing on a strategic level requires. GRIDS was a better instrument in that regard. However, almost all schools which I met putting it to serious use found that by the time they had reached about the end of Stage 3 in the process, the process itself seemed to have exhausted the energies of the staff.

This may have been a failing of the way the process was actually managed from the beginning, but I do not think so. I met several very effective deputy heads and senior teachers who were very committed to the GRIDS process. They seemed also to be capable managers. I have to conclude therefore that the problem lay within the process itself.

The only assumption I can derive from that which is relevant here is that the process attempted to provide staff with too much detail. It tried, in the best interests of busy teachers, to give schools a very precise, step-by-step procedure to follow. Was this what 'wore out' teachers' interest? I don't know. What I do know is that the systems analysis approach need not have that failing although, as I imply above, wrongly applied it could do. This is how I suggest that pitfall can be avoided.

Step 1

The top four strategic databases should be used to define four different small (two or three persons) groups of staff and 'others' (see the next section of this chapter) who will conduct a rapid (maximum of two 90-minute meetings) brainstorm of the elements in each of those four aspects of the school's strategic position. The participants in these four small brainstorming groups can use the time between their two meetings to talk to other colleagues about the factors revealed by their first review of their chosen aspect, and so check their views against those of others. If they use the SWOT format as a structure for gathering, recording and presenting their findings the whole strategic position of the school can be captured within the space of three to four weeks with between eight and twelve staff accepting a temporary but bearable addition to their workload and everyone else being involved only in brief conversations at convenient moments. And yet the sense of involvement is still both real and widely felt.

Step 2

The findings of these four groups (collated by the school's/college's senior team), should then be presented in written form to the whole staff, with the invitation to comment on any or all of them (again in writing).

This paper may also be used to ask staff to respond (if they wish) to the invitation 'What do *you* think the future might look like in general for schools like ours (a) in three to five years' time and (b) in ten+ years' time? Please give us any example(s) of key features which, from the perspective of your job/role in the school, you believe may be significantly different in the future.'

Step 3

It is then the job of a further small task group, convened and mandated by the school's most senior managers (but ideally not made up of them alone), to construct from all the staff returns a 'final' version of the school's strategic position: a summation of the SWOT analyses of the markets, business environment/competitor information, products and current resources databases together with a *forecast* of the possible futures the school/college may face.

Despite my use of the word summation this exercise should not just lead to a slavish amalgamation or précis of the contributions of others. It is a creative task which should take into account all the views expressed but should also call upon the experience and judgement of those involved in the selection and emphasis of the key influences which to them look likely to shape the school's future.

The task group then needs to analyse the range of information and opinion it has gathered in order to determine its conclusions. To achieve this the group will need to discern the underlying *assumptions* which they derive from the input (their conclusions from the review of the Strategic Positioning of the school/college), which in turn will provide the output of this part of the analysis – the *guidelines* for the reconsideration and possible refinement of the school's/college's core purpose and main objectives.

This process establishes the broad strategy for the school's further development and, conducted as recommended above, achieves this within the consciousness of all concerned.

This strategy should then be presented in terms of its key objectives, framed within a statement (or restatement) of the school's overarching purpose. With the addition of possible alternative actions by which each of the key objectives may be addressed and the preliminary estimate of relevant costs, this document, the school's 'Draft Strategic Plan', can then be discussed by all the school's key stakeholders (staff and governors especially but wherever possible representatives of the pupils and parents too).

Time expenditure needed for Steps 2 and 3

The preparation of the paper needed for Step 2 is a one to two hour task for one or two members of the senior team. A week should then be allowed for the returns from the whole staff on the initial SWOT analysis and 'futures' question to come in. Step 3 should take no more than two (90-minute) meetings of the task group, with some time (say two weeks) allowed between the two for reading and possible consultation with any individuals whose views seem of particular interest or need clarification.

Step 4

Thereafter the process of finalising the strategic plan:

● selecting the preferred actions and confirming the estimates of cost and
● adding the contingency plans and fixing review procedures/dates,

is a matter for the task group alone. Once it has been submitted to those whose formal approval and/or support is required (such as the school/college governing body) the whole plan is communicated to all who were previously involved.

Overall timescale

The whole process – with the various meetings and consultation periods planned and dated well in advance – can be completed within one school term. Conducted with slightly less pressure it can obviously fit more comfortably into a term and a half. A longer overall timescale than that should be avoided. Impetus and the sense of involvement is lost if the final plan does not emerge within something like the suggested time frame.

Individual time commitments

It is important to note that the use of this approach to structure the involvement of the whole-school community in the discernment and delineation of the school's strategic direction need not be a massive extra time commitment for any one individual. Clearly the members of the final task group will have to contribute the most time. Even their contribution is not excessive, especially when it is taken into account that much of the activity they undertake for this purpose will at least supplement and in some instances replace other routine management action on their part. Handled in the ways described this Systems Analysis approach to strategic development is not entirely an add-on to normal school routines. For example, the various necessary meetings can (should) be fitted into the school's normal calendar of formal group communication so that the time set aside within people's work-loads is in this way recycled rather than added to.

'Other' Perspectives

A further refinement of the process of collecting the data is to seek the views of people who can best be described in the working contexts of the school/college as 'significant others'. In one sense this source of data is the most authentic available. This is because a major part of any school's day-to-day existence (and therefore of its strategic position) is the place it occupies in the *perceptions* of people who have dealings with it, either as internal partners or as part of its local community. This range of people is what is meant by 'significant others', with significant referring to the directness of their experience of some aspect of the school's work/life. Examples of people who contribute to the school's strategic position via their perceptions of the school (and their communication of these to other interested parties) are as follows.

Obvious (and possibly essential) internal examples

- chair of governors/other actual governors;
- chair of PTA and other PTA members;
- individual parents who are particularly active/articulate;
- senior pupils, ie those who have been in the school for some time.

Other less obvious (external) examples

- the editor of the local paper – as a local opinion-former;
- heads/principals of other local schools/colleges – either as co-workers with shared views of the joint task of educating the community, or as competitors (whether jealous, patronising or more open in their response);
- local business leaders – as employers of ex-pupils;

- the school's immediate local neighbours – as observers/judges of the
  school via the behaviour/demeanour of pupils on the way to/from school
  (the 'crisp packets in my garden' group).

The advantage of using such people in gathering data on the school's strategic
position lies in the alternative nature of their perceptions of the school,
whether these are positive or negative. Their views are never proven facts to
be taken at face value. Their usefulness lies in their providing different
measures (standards of judgement) against which to set the school's own
experience of itself.

An illustration of this occurred when I was about to take up my headship
and was looking for a house near the school. The estate agent driving my wife
and me to look at the first property we were to see (and not knowing why we
were moving to the area) asked whether we had children. When we replied
'Yes' she continued 'Oh well, you'll like this house, it's near the best school in
the town, Angam and Flogham High School. I wouldn't advise living where
I do. The school near me is a real mess: the kids are awful.' My wife, who has
always been more confident in these respects than I and knowing I had not
been accorded the distinction of being appointed head of A and F, asked the
obvious question, 'Oh: which school is that?' The answer revealed that this
deplorable institution was not the one at which I was to become the head.
Further conversation revealed two things. The estate agent lived directly
across the road from the gates of her nearest secondary school, a very effective
ex-secondary modern, now a comprehensive which had a good team of staff,
the best head (as I came to believe later) in the town and the usual mix of keen
and creative and not so keen and occasionally resistant pupils. Our informant
definitely suffered from the 'crisp packets in the garden' syndrome. Her other
revelation, when asked what she thought of the other secondary schools in
the town and the one to which I was bound in particular, was that A and F
was the only really good school; the rest, apart from her personal near
neighbour, were just about OK. However, that same evening, unaccompa-
nied on this occasion, we visited another property in a village on the edge of
the town where the householder greeted us on the doorstep with the immediate question, 'Why are you moving down here?' This was a simpler, more
open question than the earlier one in the estate agent's car so I replied this
time. 'I'm going to be the head of Commset School in Newtown.' The reaction
to this was surprisingly gratifying. 'Oh do sit down, please. I must bring my
wife to meet you. She used to be a teacher and she thinks that's one of the
best schools in England.'

I drew several useful lessons from these exchanges. Reputation is a volatile
thing: the nearer you are to a school the more likely it is that you will see, and
dwell on, its negative features. Further away a somewhat historical, national
reputation persisted, perhaps helped by the fact that the persons concerned

had direct personal interest in the kind of work the school had pioneered. It also struck me as odd that although we had never mentioned the age of our children (a ten year old and two seven year olds at the time) our first informant had assumed we would only be concerned about the secondary sector.

For the purposes of illustrating this section, however, my real learning occurred later when I realised that just knowing the potential strength of feelings and opinions in the immediate local community, and the quirky bases on which they could be formed, provided a useful yardstick against which to measure some of our more esoteric ideas concerning our further development. 'Not losing sight of the knitting' was a graphic phrase I heard an American principal use to describe a similar realisation he and his staff had stumbled upon when in attempting to brainstorm the best possible future for their college, only to realise later how far their views had drifted from the expectations of key groups of others involved.

One tip, if you decide to seek the perceptions of one or more of these 'others' as a contribution to the Strategic Positioning exercise, is to offer them some kind of simple structure through which to do this. Using the SWOT analysis is the most straightforward I have come across. Inviting someone to jot down under the four headings (on one side of A4 paper) what they consider to be the school's strengths and weaknesses as seen from their particular standpoint, and whether they can suggest any opportunities of which they think the school might take advantage or any threats they think it might face in the future, is infinitely more helpful, to them and to you, than saying something like, 'Do you mind telling me what you think of the school?' Although the more open invitation might produce a richer crop of opinion, if you had the time and proper opportunity to process it, you seldom have that kind of luxury. It is better to frame the time and level of commitment to the task demanded of both parties in some way. The best version of this I have come across was from a local drug company, for whom I chaired an 'ethics' committee for some time. It sent me four postcards, each with a straightforward question about the company typed on it; responding to the question on each card and returning them in the envelope provided was a very painless way of lending my support to their strategic review.

Three 'Don'ts'

Don't 'leave it to the planning department'

This is an unlikely scenario in schools and colleges. Except in the largest it is unlikely that a specific 'Strategic Planning Department' would ever be set up. But that is exactly what happened in many British companies in the late 1950s when our home industries 'discovered' strategic planning across the water in the USA and brought it home to use. Specialist planners were trained and set up, as a further adjunct to already complicated, hierarchical management structures, in their own department. After the first flush of enthusiasm for the ideas they brought and the questions they asked, company after company found that in succeeding years everyone else 'left it to the planning department'. As a result, strategic development became isolated from the concerns of those whose daily actions actually give life to the strategy, the procedures for devising and defining strategy became more and more bureaucratic and, ultimately, its impact on the growth of the company was nil.

Even if the vast majority of schools/colleges are never likely to have a planning department, if the Systems Analysis approach ever becomes seen as the particular province of one or two people in the school the same tendency to 'leave it to them: my job's to teach' will emerge and the values which I believe make this a planning tool of real potential will be lost.

Note: That is not the effect if the Systems Analysis model is used as suggested at the start of this chapter, by the head/principal or some other senior member of staff, simply to structure her/his/their own thinking on more strategic lines. Used in this way no other colleagues are drawn explicitly into a new process which has been given the fancy new name of 'Systems Analysis' and expected to build it into their own thinking about their jobs. Hence the danger of 'leaving it to the planning department' does not arise.

Don't worry about the 'ten+ year' vision of the future

Many people to whom I have introduced this approach as part of a training programme have said things like, 'Ten years: ha! Don't ask me what the school might be like in ten years, I'm not that sure what it will be like in two or three years.' That reaction was particularly prevalent during the early, halcyon days of the introduction of the National Curriculum, when government-established bodies seemed to change their minds more frequently than horses change their shoes.

The point is that unless we force ourselves to make some sort of estimate, however imaginary, of what the school might be doing/might have to be responding to that far ahead we will more than likely miss some key development until it is almost too late. Our thinking about strategy will be dominated by our concerns for the present and the immediate, foreseeable future. To refer for the last time to the presenter through whom I first met this approach, when answering a riposte similar to that quoted above he said 'My company always looks at least ten years ahead, it has to. But we check our broadest assumptions about the future at least once every year and conduct a more formal version of this whole process approximately every five years.' In other words 'ten years' is far enough ahead to make us *imagine*; and that kind of imagining does not commit us to irrevocable action until we have had the opportunity to check out our assumptions as the future unfolds. Ten years ahead then becomes a constantly moving, distant goal which can only be imprecisely perceived but is essential if we seek a genuinely strategic dimension for the school's/college's continuous development.

And finally remember – Don't be slavish

This is a particular danger in the case of a diagrammatic model such as that presented by Figure 3.1. The very lines of each of the boxes can suggest a separation between the features they represent which is unlike the complex, confused and sometimes ambiguous reality of a school/college. So be prepared, as I suggested earlier, once the approach and its intentions have been fully understood, to use the approach with imagination. Respect its basic methodological stance, seek to apply each part of it to the analysis of your own school but do so imaginatively with an eye to the organic wholeness of your own organisation.

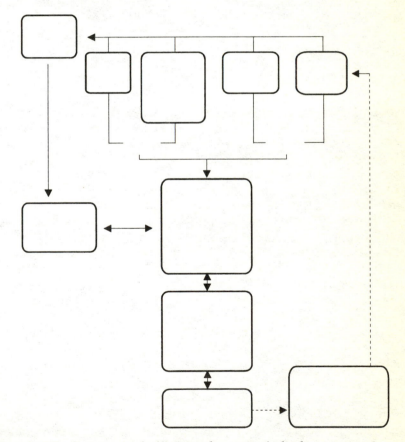

Figure 3.1 *The Systems Analysis approach – strategic databases*

4

Avoiding Own Goals: The Customer Approach to Strategic Development Planning

～

Who (or what) is a Customer?

The next part of my story about strategic planning describes an approach which depends greatly (as you can see from the title to this chapter) upon the potential value of *metaphor* in helping each of us promote that unlocking of our understanding of our own existing practices, and the effective reappraisal of these, which is the necessary corollary of any form of truly strategic development. However, in deliberately proposing this approach which depends for its efficacy on the value of metaphor I was reminded of an article (Beavis and Thomas, 1996) which pointed to what the authors (two university teachers in Australia) rightly see as a danger in this use of metaphor.

Confirming first my own experience of the value of metaphor in the process of learning from organisational experience, they remind us that 'Metaphors... enable a transference of meaning from one action or experience to another to which such meaning does not literally apply. The advantage is... that insight from one entity can be used in conceptualising the other.' However, they go on to show that the unrestrained, and often unconscious, use of metaphors from organisational cultures alien to our own, educational one leads inevitably to the indiscriminate importing of *expectations* from those other cultures which 'may well lead to a distorted view of reality by associations that are unhelpful.' Their particular worry is that the use of factory metaphors such as 'the end-product of schooling' and 'learning outcomes' can lead to expectations of uniformity, competition and conveyor belts which are inappropriate in schools/colleges. It was a similar concern that made me write at some length earlier on the possible interpretations of profit in educational organisations and to take some pains to distinguish myself from those who might make the mistake of confusing pupils with products. Yet it was my conviction that there is an opposite and equal danger – that we in education may ignore the learning which can be derived from seeking to make an accurate, if analogous, translation of such alien concepts into our world – which led me to recommend that we should take even the concept of profit seriously enough to examine its possible import for us.

Thus while remaining alive to the inherent dangers of metaphors drawn originally from organisational cultures different from our own I believe we have much to learn about our organisations from their use. 'They open up the multi-dimensional space necessary for the comprehension of the social reality in which we live, and they mediate that reality so as to enable us to [think] in ways that may not have been possible within a more literal under-standing of [that] reality' (Beavis and Thomas, 1996).

So my contention is that for our purposes the very fact of forcing ourselves to revisit and review our own practices in language developed in other working contexts is a potential source of benefit. It makes us ask questions of ourselves and the practices we adopt which are far less likely to be posed if we remain within our traditional educational lexicon. Provided we continu-ally check that our own fundamental values and purposes are still in place the dangers posed by manufacturing or business metaphors can be ade-quately dealt with while we take advantage of the insights they provide.

This balance, between the danger and the advantage of metaphor, has to be especially sought in the case of this next approach, which depends funda-mentally upon our use and interpretation of the word 'customer'. 'Customer' is a word with which I am personally very comfortable, because it serves to draw into my mind a particular view of organisations to which I respond with total confidence. On the other hand I know that many others with whom I work in schools/colleges still find it a difficult word to use without believing (as Beavis and Thomas' work confirms) that they are intrinsically changing their expectations of themselves and of their work from a pupil-centred, educational perspective to one more redolent of the business world.

There are also, perhaps more worryingly, a few with whom I work who accept the customer terminology more readily than even I would wish. I suspect this is because they welcome the metaphoric shift towards business parameters for its own sake. Returning however to those (the legitimately doubting majority) who do not find themselves happy with a word like customer I must explain the view of organisations which gives me the reverse of their doubts – the unshakeable conviction that seeing one's job in education (and therefore seeing the work of schools in the round) in terms of customers is what, more than any other single factor, helps me translate into education-ally valuable concepts the realities of life inside organisations and, in particu-lar, the responses and responsibilities of management and leadership which those realities demand. The concepts which help me formulate this conviction come from the work of W Edwards Deming, the American expert in the management of organisations who died in 1994.

Deming's view of an organisation is essentially a straightforward one. It derives from his belief that any organisation is simply a group of individuals in pursuit of a common purpose which is achieved by a series of interlinked processes, each of which is controlled either by one of those individuals (eg a tutor completing a set of reports or a teacher delivering a lesson) or by groups of them (eg a pastoral or departmental team meeting to discuss and determine a new tutorial policy or a common system for marking and assessment). For each of these processes there are a series of inputs – things which must be in place to allow that process to take place effectively. In the case of the tutor completing her reports a sufficient quantity of blank report forms for her own comments and the information she requires from other teachers to complete the report on each student are both examples of the inputs necessary for her to conduct the process of 'report completion'. Once she has done the reports there is an output – a completed set of reports for her form or tutorial group. Now the problem of metaphor is even worse isn't it? All this use of 'input' and 'output' brings the business (even the factory) images still closer; but for a worthwhile purpose I believe, so suspend your disbelief a little longer. The culminating element to this part of Deming's view of organisations is as follows.

Given this micro-level view of an organisation (in terms of the myriad of individual processes by which it meets the common purpose which is its *raison d'être*) he then points out that the concept of 'customer' is absolutely fundamental to the effective working of any organisation. A 'customer' in Deming's terms is anyone who is dependent on the output of someone else's process so that she or he can get on with his or her own (process). Internal to the organisation this will be a further step in the overall series of processes which go to make up the organisation's total output – its achievement of the overall purpose which brings it together as an organisation. Externally of course the customers are those who are relying on the output of the organisation in order to make use of it to meet whatever are their own needs/purposes (eg a student requiring qualifications to enter higher education or one needing the enrichment and development of personal values and enthusiasms provided by the school/college in order to take full advantage of her or his individual talents).

In the example above of the tutor with a set of reports to complete, when she is about to begin her process she is the customer of those who must provide the inputs which are essential to her task – those who order and distribute the report forms and those of her colleagues who must provide the information she needs to complete her reports. In completing her task she in turn has a customer (or customers) awaiting the output of her process in order to complete theirs: probably whichever member(s) of the senior management of the school/college whose job it is to read the reports, add their comments and countersign the reports.

This explanation of the concept of customer provides for me a better basic model of organisations than any other I know. It stresses the centrality of *mutual interdependence* which I perceive at work in every effective school or college I visit. It also reveals how (and why) *every single process* in a school/college *should be valued equally*, regardless of the spurious status which is often attached to one part of the overall process over another: the cleanliness of a classroom as one of the essential contributions to a good environment for learning is placed on an organisational par with the quality of the teaching necessary to convert that room into a place of excitement and wonder. I believe those are educationally valuable perspectives worthy of attention by all of us. For me they derive directly from Deming's view of organisations and his response to the question, 'Who is my customer?' To Deming there is only one awesomely simple answer to that query: 'Whoever has to wait for me to do my job well so that they can get on with whatever it is they have to/wish to do next'.

Deming on Management

This is another Deming concept central to this customer-driven view of organisations. Deming's definition of the basic purpose of management in any organisation matches his chosen organisational model with equal simplicity. He points out that each of the separate processes necessary to enable the organisation to meet its core purposes has to be connected by *systems* to the other processes which go to make up the whole. It is the peculiar role of management to manage the connections between the various processes, and especially to manage the interconnection of the people with the systems, to ensure that the systems enable the people to succeed. To Deming therefore management is not (or should not be) a top down control mechanism; its crucial function is to enable the organisation as a whole to work effectively. Furthermore, management – in the Deming sense – is not simply the province of those with senior status, it is the proper concern of everyone: at the most basic levels of operation everyone is responsible for managing the immediate interconnection between her or his process and the 'customer' who awaits the output of that process so she or he can carry out the process for which she or he is responsible. Reviving the earlier example of the tutor and her reports, and placing it firmly in a secondary school context, any subject teacher who fails to meet the deadline for completing her subject reports has failed to manage the interconnection to her customer/colleague, the tutor. Similarly, if the tutor does not ensure that her comments are in place by the deadline set then she will have failed to manage the interconnection to her senior colleague who has to await the arrival of the set of reports before being able to complete the process (of reading and countersigning) for which she is responsible. Nevertheless there are extra, system-wide duties for those who have accepted this responsibility, those who are traditionally termed 'senior management' (thus incarnating both the hierarchical and control-focused view which dominates our usual interpretation of management as a whole). In the series of interconnections suggested by the example a crucial responsibility of 'senior management' is to ensure that the relevant deadlines and provision of basic resources are all in place to enable the various teachers involved to each manage their own process effectively. Thus setting the deadline for completion by the form teacher only 24 hours after she is expected to receive the last of the comments from her subject teacher colleagues would be one example of mismanagement of their system-wide responsibility by the senior management.

Once again I find this whole perspective on management entirely congruent with my view of educational organisations and their intrinsic purposes. It stresses mutuality and interconnectedness, not seniority or status, while making it clear that those who accept special responsibilities (such as heads of department, subject co-ordinators, deputies and heads/principals) have a primary duty to ensure continually that the systems they put in place actually *enable* those others who have to carry out each individual part of the process.

These are the concepts and values which, despite the dangers of using metaphor alluded to above, bring me to recommend to you this second approach to strategic development planning. It focuses on this concept of customer and in particular, for our purposes of strategic planning, on a school's/college's perception of the objectives held by its various external customer groups.

The Customer Approach to Strategic Planning

Now that the particular concept of customer on which this approach is built has been etablished it is a relatively straightforward one to explain. Unsurprisingly, given my concern to lock our interpretation of strategic planning to an understanding of the fundamentals which drive any organisation as they relate to the range of possible futures it may face, it also has conceptual and practical aspects which are similar to the previous model (set out in Chapters 2 and 3). This should help keep the exposition to more reasonable proportions than might otherwise have been the case.

Once again I set out first the linear version of the steps which comprise this model as I first met them. On this occasion a colleague and I were in the position of the client, seeking the help of a consultant experienced in this field. We had a brief from our sponsors, the LEAs who had each pooled a proportion of their in-service monies to create the three-year project which was our organisational setting. Broadly, our purpose was to research more cost-effective ways of providing training and support for management development for school managers in all the schools across the region covered by the sponsoring LEAs. We asked our consultant contact for help in framing an explicit strategy through which to meet our professional and contractual responsibilities.

It should be noted that I first met this approach when having to devise a strategy *ab initio* rather than from a review of existing structures and disposition of resources. Nevertheless I have worked since with several schools who have made use of this approach, adapted to suit their own needs, in moving their existing systems and structures forward on a more coherent, strategic basis. The basic mind-set to adopt is to assume the school/college is starting from scratch and therefore looking towards an entirely new future, and then respond to each of the prompts provided by the model below accordingly, using the data from your existing systems as appropriate but in this essentially future-related context. One clear advantage of this approach is that by adopting this starting point you will find it far more natural and straightforward to include projections of possible alternative futures, for instance changes in the kinds of customers you will have caused by the introduction of new forms of schooling in your area (eg the reintroduction of selection), or changes in the external operational contexts such as that brought about when the different funding arrangements were introduced for the further education/6th form college sector. However, even if you don't predict quite such significant external changes for your school/college, this approach will still provide another valuable way of appraising and reassessing what you do, and why, with a view to developing it further at a strategic level.

The linear model of the approach

1. The core purpose (*raison d'être*) of the organisation.
2. The organisation (its owners/members/policy makers – the internal stakeholders).
3. The external customers of the organisation.
4. End objectives of each group of the organisation's external customers
5. Analysis of resources available.
6. The organisation's own objectives.
   - Overall policy aims (fundamental purposes of internal stakeholders)
   - For each objective, action plans, including: actions; relevance to policy; assumptions.
7. Check-list (to cross reference customer objectives with organisational goals/targets).

Addressing the linear model as a school/college

Each stage in the process described by the linear model can be usefully framed as a question, cast in the contexts of schools/colleges.

1. What is our school/college primarily for? (ie what, overall, does it exist to achieve?)
2. When we talk of 'the school' or 'the college' (as an organisation striving to achieve or provide something) which group(s) of people do we have in mind as comprising it and what (different?) 'stake' does each of these groups have in it?
3. Which groups of people are we thinking of when we consider those towards whom our achievements and the provision we make are directed? Who do we see as our 'customers'?
4. What does each of those groups expect or want from us? What are *their* objectives for our school/college?
5. What do our resources make possible? What staffing, accommodation, money, time do we have?
6. What do we *want* to do?
   - What is our understanding of our overall 'mission' as a school/college?
   - How do we go or intend to go about achieving it? What do we actually do or intend to do?
   - How closely does each chosen approach demonstrate our commitment to our mission?
   - What assumptions can we make about the likely impact of each of our chosen approaches?
7. Can we now map each of our customers' objectives against each major strand of our activity as a school/college to see how closely they match?

Each of these questions is designed to address the *fundamentals* of the school's/college's approach to its overall task as an educational institution. As such the responses should aim to meet two criteria in each case: they should be simple and they should be strategic. In order to achieve this you need to avoid the temptation to embellish any particular response with too much detail. Many-layered responses, beloved of all of us who work in the education field (particularly when we are asked to explain precisely what we are doing or why) are best avoided as being too complex to serve our purpose here. What we are looking for is a response which is fine-tuned to the essentials that provide the skeleton behind the flesh of everything we do.

Yet in searching for these simple, uni-dimensional responses which will reveal (to us) the core of our understanding, the instinctive beliefs and values which prompt our actions, we must also be careful not to fall into the trap of blandness. Our responses must be penetrative as well as straightforward if they are to help us devise (or redevise) our strategy on the basis of those fundamentals which shape our organisational realities. To this end the next chapter presents the same principles, of a customer-driven approach to strategy development, but in a reordered form.

Proforma for recording a first-level response to the customer approach to strategic planning

1. What is our school/college for?

2. Of whom is it comprised? (Who is responsible for it? Who has a stake in it?)

3. Who are our customers?

4. What do (each of) those customers want from us?

5. What resources do we have at our disposal?

6. What do we (ie those listed in answer to question 2) want or intend to do?

7. How will our various customers' wishes and expectations (question 4) be met by our desired or intended courses of action (question 6)? (Are any not met? Are we doing or planning to do things which don't appear to meet any clearly defined customer needs or demands?)

This is followed by some further teasing-out of each of the questions above. By these means I am attempting to draw more specific connections between the intended focus of each question and the kind of response to it which is required in order to help us frame our strategy. In this way I hope to share my own experience of meeting this approach for the first time, as these are the kinds of questions and probings it provoked in me.

Before going on to Chapter 5, however, my suggestion is that you draw up a first-level response for yourself to each of the questions posed above. For ease of reference these are presented again in a form which may be photocopied and enlarged to provide a simple proforma for completion.

My suggestion is that you complete this first-level response quickly, giving your instinctive reactions to the prompt provided by each question, and not attempting to add too much detail at this stage. This is particularly true in the case of question 5 (resources), where you simply need to make sure you capture all the possible sources and give a broad indication of the total provision available from each of them in order to summarise for yourself the range of resource on which you can call to meet your chosen purposes.

5

Matching Customer Expectation with Professional Judgement: The Strategic Challenge for Every School/College

Despite the somewhat lengthy preamble to this second, alternative way of approaching strategic planning with which I opened the last chapter I believe that many readers may still find the whole concept of 'customer' an uncomfortable one. The potentially negative implications of this metaphor for them will override my own convictions. For that reason this chapter presents an alternative view which I have found helpful when using this approach in workshop situations.

On this occasion let's begin with my visual representation of this view which helps explain the peculiar advantages this approach brought for me.

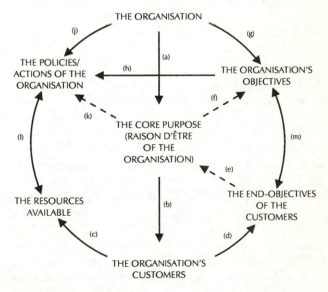

Figure 5.1 *An alternative approach*

Explanations

1. Apart from an instinctive preference for diagrams which owe more to circles than straight lines the importance, to me, of this view of the 'customer approach' to strategic planning lies in the way that it presents what I see as the essential points of interrelationship between the various key influences on any organisation's strategic approach to its task.

2. The placement of the various elements of the diagram in relation to each other is therefore significant. Does this placement seem at first sight to be meaningful to you? If not what amendments would you make and why?

   These are not meant to be idle, space-filling questions. Asking them allows me to invite you once again to make your own sense out of my view of this bit of the world of schools and their strategic development. Also if you do find it best to make adjustments to this model in my experience that will itself have involved you in a closer engagement with the ideas on which it is based than any amount of further description and explanation would achieve.

3. However, before finalising any adjustments you wish to make to the diagram, I recommend paying especial attention to the arrowed lines. The directions of the arrows is obviously an important part of the model. As you can see most of them are uni-directional; crucially two are not. What I am attempting to represent to myself is how I believe this approach invites us to regard the development of strategy for an organisation in practice.

The arrowed lines

Lines [a] to [e]

Although the core purpose of the organisation should (I believe) be at the centre of the whole process, this has to be derived [line a] from the organisation whose members determine for what reason (or purpose) they, as an organisation, exist. This core purpose, in turn, helps determine who are the 'customers' of the organisation [b]. Parents and pupils choosing a comprehensive school rather than the locally available alternative which selects pupils on the basis of exam performance at age 11 do so because they are responding to the comprehensive school's *raison d'être* (its intention to admit and educate all pupils who wish to attend, regardless of the level of their achievement at age 11); and vice versa of course. Perhaps more frequently than we would care to admit a school's/college's selection of its purpose (and the ethos that results from this) influences the nature of its customer base negatively more than positively; parents who do not approve send their offspring to other schools where that option is open to them.

Whichever of these scenarios prevails parents/pupils are the source [c] of the major part of the school's resources; personally in the case of fee-paying schools/colleges in the independent sector or via some public authority in the case of maintained sector schools.

However, each of these customers (as individuals and/or groups) as well as responding to the school's/college's overall purpose also bring to their relationship with the organisation their own set of objectives [d].

Over time these *may* (hence the diagonal dotted line [e] in the south-east corner) help shape or refine the organisation's core purpose. More immediately they create demands or expectations which, sometimes explicitly but more frequently in my experience less overtly, the customers expect will influence the objectives by which the schools go about fulfilling their core purpose. An example of this would be a parental demand for the introduction of a specific subject on to the curriculum which a school/college decides not to introduce (say a foreign language in a primary school or an extra A-level or GNVQ in a sixth form).

Lines [f] to [k]

Meanwhile the organisation should, logically, derive [f] its own objectives from its chosen core purpose, since they will be the means by which that purpose is achieved. However, in practice any organisation's objectives are also derived *directly from the individual and collective preferences* of key members of the organisation [g] without conscious reference to its core purpose.

However they are arrived at it is clearly the objectives of the organisation (the individual things it wants to achieve) which determine [h] its policies and actions. Less obviously however (usually in reaction to a set of unforeseen circumstances) the actions and sometimes even the policies of the organisation arise directly from the actual behaviours of its key members [j]. This may occur without reference to any specific objective, but possibly (hence the dotted arrow in the north-western sector of the diagram [k]) in some instinctive way linked to or motivated by a sense of part of the organisation's core purpose, often its desire simply to survive.

Lines [l] and [m]

And so, finally, to the two bi-directional lines; the one on the left [l] is largely self-explanatory. Resources predominantly influence (enable or curtail) the range of actions an organisation can take. However, the careful selection and planned deployment of the available resources (determined by the choice of policies and actions an organisation makes) also affects the degree to which the resources meet the purposes of the organisation. This is what the current framework for the inspection of schools is seeking to establish under the broad heading 'value for money' within the 'efficiency of the school' aspect of the Office for Standards in Education (Ofsted) framework for the inspection of schools. In short a school's chosen paths of action may be wasteful (thus diminishing the total amount of resource at its disposal) or efficient (thus adding value to the original amounts of resource available to it).

Line [m] is for me the most important part of this whole approach. The objectives of an organisation, whether derived via an interpretation of its core purpose or directly from the preferences of its key members, *should* be influenced by the end objectives of the customers. This is not, in these days of the increasingly damaging competition between schools and colleges, just one more version of the free marketeers' doctrinal view of the 1990s world of organisations – 'keep your customers happy or they'll go elsewhere'. There is clearly something of that view which no school/college may afford to ignore, unless perhaps it is in the very rare situation of being the only educational option open to pupils and parents within a very broad geographical area.

Of much more importance is the fact that unless a school/college actively seeks to ensure that its objectives meet most of the end objectives of its customers, it will fall into a mode of operation far worse than that in which schools find themselves who follow only the arid ethic of the 'free' marketplace.

A school/college that pays no attention to the wishes of its customers, which follows exclusively its own pattern of priority and preference, ignoring the expectations of those whose presence provides its *raison d'être*, can succeed only in terms of self-gratification. Even if that gratification is based on apparently high professional ideals and intentions this does not seem to me to be an acceptable goal for any educational institution. To succeed in meeting one's own objectives while failing to meet those of the people towards whom one's professional activities are directed seems so unlikely as to be impossible to conceive. Is it therefore just plain foolish to describe such a seemingly hypothetical situation, or is it stupidly sensible (an oxymoron in the best Greek tradition) to do so? I believe it is the latter.

It is of course such a highly unlikely scenario in terms of the whole of the offering made by any school or college as to make reference to it virtually absurd. Conversely, however, it is a very likely scenario to encounter within significant parts of that offering. Experiences in my own and in many other schools have shown me that while schools and colleges (and most teachers who work in them) strive hard to work for the benefit of pupils/students, their definition of what they should strive to achieve for and with those pupils/students is very frequently so one-sided as to eliminate any possible sense of the objective sought being a shared one.

The examples one sees of this are of individual wishes or demands of one pupil failing to be met because they do not match the current offering made by the school, often associated with the finite nature of the resources available.

A school refusing to run a Year 10/11 option group just for one or two pupils is one such example. These situations must be expected wherever the resources made available are predicated upon a delivery system based on groups: it is impossible to guarantee every individual choice other than on the basis of a one-to-one tutorial system. Where these occur they are not therefore examples of failure by schools or colleges in themselves. Nevertheless even in these numerically explicable situations I have observed some where I would consider the school blameworthy for its wilful insistence on pursuing its own purposes. An example occurred when I saw what would now be a Year 9 pupil forced to accept Technical Drawing as an 'option' because 'all the other sets in that block are full'; and this by a school which at the time boasted in its literature of the '49 options offered to all pupils'.

More significant in the context of this approach to strategic planning are the greater number of instances where schools demonstrate a more general unconcern for (or at least a lack of awareness of) the objectives of their customers and insist on their own view prevailing. One of the most prevalent examples comes from my memories of parents' evenings which were so widespread in the maintained (secondary) sector throughout the 1960s and 1970s, and there follows an anecdotal illustration of the (unintended) consequences of this exclusive determination of professional objectives.

At such evenings I became used to hearing teachers saying to parents things like, 'in my professional opinion...' or, 'I'm sorry if I can't make you understand but you'll just have to trust us' or 'Don't worry, we know what we're doing.' It would be inaccurate to claim that every time I heard one of those kinds of phrases the teacher concerned was entirely ignoring the objectives the parents wished the school to pursue in that situation in favour of her or his own preferences. Nor am I saying that even where this was the case the teachers concerned were consciously choosing such a path.

However, I have experienced a sufficient number of these 'the school/the teacher knows best' reactions to gauge that many of them arose as the inevitable result of a failure to address the key concept on which this approach focuses; namely that in the formulation of its objectives (its choice of alternative ways of fulfilling its core purpose) any organisation (and most of all a school/college) needs to take active cognisance of its customers' needs or wishes (their 'end objectives' as this model terms them). If parents wish to be told clearly and to understand fully what the school or teacher is saying about their child then to stop short of reaching these ends in favour of meeting one of your own (even if it was the eminently reasonable one of moving on to the next parents) has to be questionable in an organisational context in which the needs of the individual are supposedly of prime concern.

I have chosen this most mundane example of what I see to be the endemic professional error revealed by this approach in order to try and demonstrate the unwitting but damaging pitfalls which can occur if we do not, at the more strategic levels at least, give active consideration to the need to review the match between our preferred objectives and those of our customers. I have witnessed sufficient such examples to convince me that this approach to the review and development of strategy offers a valuable antidote to such a tendency, as well as providing a usable planning tool overall.

However, the interconnecting line in this part of the model is double ended. One of the most distinguishing features of education organisations is that as well as having regard to their customer's end objectives they also have the responsibility of responding to these in the light of their own professional experience and judgement. In some cases 'school' will 'know best' and any attempt simply to follow slavishly the demands of the customer would be irresponsible. An example of this faced by most schools from time to time is an expectation of the head, by parents, that disruptive pupils (the sons or daughters of other parents) will be excluded so that 'their' children can get on. It is a reasonable enough expectation when viewed from the perspective of the individual parent whose child is not disruptive. The school however has to act on behalf of *all* its pupils, a requirement which bars it from meeting this particular parental objective on every occasion, even if the request in itself is reasonable enough.

That example also illustrates another, associated difficulty of the customer-led approach – the inevitable clash between the end objectives of one customer and another. Reduced to individual levels, any situation of disruptive pupil behaviour is likely to involve conflicting demands (end objectives) from different sets of parents. This particular approach does not pretend that in such individual circumstances the school/college *has* to satisfy both sets of conflicting objectives: though many heads/principals wear themselves out attempting (very properly) to do just that.

What this approach *is* seeking to make us explore here is the degree of coherence (match) between the school's/college's objectives and the broad end objectives sought by different groups of its customers. A better example of where a school may have to follow its own professional judgement against the expressed desires of at least a significant group of its customers arose with the curriculum choice of a secondary school to move to dual-award (or combined science) for all pupils, when many parents expressed a strong preference to retain the three separate science options of the previous system. A primary sector example of a similar nature was the refusal by a junior school – despite strong parental pressure – to introduce formal language teaching before Year 6.

Whatever our personal views of the merits of the individual school's decision in either of those examples I believe that they represent areas where the school may claim a legitimate supremacy for its view over that of its customers. What distinguishes them from the 'In my professional opinion' and 'You'll just have to trust us' examples earlier is that it was evident in both cases that the school had taken its customers' objectives seriously, had recognised the necessity for rejection and could also demonstrate a clear rationale for it.

In other words this approach invites schools and colleges to check and recheck their chosen objectives against the yardstick provided by the end objectives of their customers. In so doing it does not suggest either that they should slavishly provide whatever their customers demand or that they can meet all the objectives of every one of the individuals who makes up their total customer group. Following one of these reactions would either be a recipe for professional abdication or a fast route to chaos. Consciously, constantly and conscientiously searching for the best balance between the two sets of objectives is what is called for, especially when a school or college is planning its broad strategies for the future.

We will now ask the questions first posed in Chapter 4 again, against this alternative model of the customer-led approach and in greater detail. You may find it helpful to have your initial responses to the questions available as you read through the more detailed versions below.

Question 1. What is our school for?

This original, linear-model version of this question gives us a clear clue as to the kind of the response which is needed here.

All schools have statements of aims and objectives; nowadays some of these are presented (following the fashion of the training models first developed for large, private sector organisations) as mission statements. The problem with most of them is that they retain much of the qualities of multiplicity and complexity which characterised the formal statements of aims and objectives produced by the educational world throughout the 1960s and 1970s. At that time schools defended both the number of their stated aims and the levels of complexity in which these were presented on the grounds that schools, as organisations, had to have many and many-layered aims in order to express properly what it was they were trying to achieve. They said that the unitary expressions of aim which they perceived being used by the business world were inapposite for schools and colleges. This perception was explained by an understandable conclusion that the only aim of all businesses was to make profits. I say understandable because most businesses did use that expression of aim very readily – particularly when justifying significant reductions in staff; many still do. As Charles Handy (1996) described it, most businesses believe that 'half the people, being paid twice as much to produce three times more, is good for everyone – except the other half of the people'. However, even if that was a fair representation of the singularity of business aims in the 1970s and 1980s, most private sector companies are now beginning to realise that profit alone is not enough: making a profit – in the simplest sense of the organisation earning more than it spends – is necessary but not sufficient. Profit is a short-term objective. If a business concentrates solely on that it leads ultimately to its own demise. This is because such singular concentration leads to a failure to invest in those aspects of any business which support its survival (and growth) in the long term – its customers and the people who work for it who provide the quality outcomes the customers desire.

Furthermore even if profit was legitimately *the* sole aim of companies there is not, and never was, any reason for schools and colleges to use that argument to resist so vehemently attempts to ask them to define *their* core purpose in more singular and fundamental terms. The reason for this is the same one that moves sensible businesses away from the position of making profit their only goal. Unless you continually define and redefine clearly what your organisation is in business for, ie what it is there to provide or achieve which would not be provided or achieved if it was not there, you are likely to confuse what you are currently doing with what you are trying to achieve; to concentrate solely on the short term. That in itself does not immediately result in a catastrophic state affairs, but it does when what you are doing (and usually have done well for several years) ceases to be the only or the best way of providing what you set out to provide.

An illustration of short-term survival objectives triumphing over a clear understanding of core purpose can be seen in the demise of British Rail (BR) as a major provider of the transportation of goods in the UK. The development of road transport systems has reduced BR's goods service from its former pre-eminence in this field. One major explanation lies in the concept that BR's management had of their core purpose over the intervening years, which on all the evidence we have, must have been something of the order of 'We're in the business of running the national railway system as cost effectively as we can.' Consider how differently they might have acted years ago if they (had they been allowed to by successive governments) had defined their core purpose as 'We're in the business of being the major provider of transportation of bulk goods in the UK.' Given this fundamental sense of purpose, instead of concentrating their energies on ways of making the railway system *as it stood* more efficient, they could have reconceived it in terms of a world in which the lorry and the aircraft were bound to play a more major role, and set about devising an integrated system involving these newer forms of transport alongside the railways. This is not to say that 'blame' for the failure to act in this way rests entirely on the British Rail management. One of the few things about the history of BR over the last 30 or so years which seems obvious to me is, as the parenthetical comment above suggested, that it has been severely constrained by successive bouts of political non- or misdirection.

What I am seeking to illustrate is the way in which a failure to define and redefine the fundamental *raison d'être* for any organisation makes probably the most significant contribution to that organisation's ultimate failure.

Schools/colleges must, if they wish to take seriously their own strategic development, be able to say with clarity and simplicity precisely what business they are in. Listing every ambition they entertain and every value they seek to meet is important, but is not what is required here. Compare the following two statements of purpose.

(a) We aim to develop the potential of every pupil to the maximum of her or his potential. We aim to:
   ● challenge our pupils to get the most out of themselves;
   ● present a curriculum which meets the needs of every pupil;
   ● help all our pupils gain the best grades of which they are capable in exams;
   ● show our pupils, by precept and example, the values of tolerance and respect for other people;
   ● instil a sense of corporate and community contribution in all our pupils;
   ● empower our pupils with the personal and interpersonal skills necessary for their participation in the economic world;
   ● provide our pupils with an understanding of the shared culture of which they are a part;
   ● demonstrate the value of hard work in pursuit of personal goals.

(b) Our job is to enable all our students to learn. We want each of them to leave us with:
   ● an in-built respect for all other peoples and the world around them;
   ● a sense of wonder at what there is still to discover, about themselves and the world;
   ● the confidence and skill to do so.

Both are excellent statements of the intentions and values of the two schools concerned. I would be happy (and proud) to work in either of them. The first is a good, composite list of most of the key areas of preoccupation which schools/colleges have to address if they are to be effective. It speaks of challenge, curriculum, exam success, tolerance, community, skills, culture and hard work. However, the very length of the list and the fact that it is predicated on that most imprecise of all school/college aspirations – maximising potential – means that *for the purpose of steering the school's overall sense of strategy* it is not sufficiently focused. It is a better, 1990s version of the vague, more rounded statements of aims and objectives which abounded in schools in the 1960s but, for the purpose of strategic development, it is still too much of a 'catch-all' expression of purpose.

For the purposes of developing the school's strategy the second is infinitely more helpful because it is focused more on the fundamentals. It says to me that this school is above all about learning, and that its concept of learning has an inescapable central thrust of self-responsibility (of the learner for herself or himself, for others and for her or his own learning). The three objectives are a consistent extension of the opening description of the school's purpose, and the wholeness of the result is as important as its brevity compared to the expression of aims from the other school. In other words, it gets to the heart of what the school is seeking to achieve more readily, and that is what is required in answer to the question, 'What is our school for?'

Question 2. 'Of whom is the school comprised? Who is responsible for it?'

This question aims to make us define clearly all those who have any significant responsibility for the school/college (and therefore for determining what it does). Except in the very small percentage of cases within the independent sector where owners and managers of private schools still persist, the answer to this question will vary greatly from school to school.

Ignoring the temptation to interpret the second part of the question wilfully in the widest possible terms so as, for instance, to include pupil responsibilities for the school (as when they are its formal or informal representation to the external world) the range of groups for immediate inclusion in response to the first part of this question seems to me to be:

- the head and staff of the school;
- the governors;
- parent representative groups;
- any group of owners in the legally constituted sense, such as the trustees of a school with charitable status.

Other groups may spring quickly to mind as you contemplate this list in the context of your own school/college: if so, add them to the list.

What is more important is to attempt to define with some care the reality of your own situation in response to the second part of the question. In this case the *legal* answer is probably an example of the 'necessary but not sufficient' condition. Throughout the maintained sector, but given peculiar emphasis in the grant maintained and post-16 parts of that sector, the school governors now have a clear legal responsibility for the school and its affairs. This has always been the case in the world of further education: it is still a much newer factor for primary and secondary schools. In the independent sector there are many variations of the bodies where legal responsibility for the school rests, all of them for purposes such as DfEE registration and school inspection by Ofsted/HMI teams described under the blanket term 'owners'.

What is vital for our purposes here is to peer both at and behind that legal screen in an attempt to discern which groups of people routinely influence the policy development of the school/college through their decisions. Some schools, usually because of the effectiveness and longstanding of the incumbent head, may still, in practice, be examples of what the legal world describes as a 'sole trader'. In such instances, now far rarer than was the case say 15 years ago, the reality is that the operational responsibility rests solely with the headteacher. Decisions, especially about change, may apparently be taken by the governors but examination of the processes by which such decisions are reached can still reveal that nothing the head has recommended or requested has, within living memory, been resisted by the governors and nothing significant has, in the same timescale, been forced on the head by them.

In other cases governors now exercise very substantial, real responsibility: in an increasing number of instances (apparent in the press from time to time) to the exclusion or at least overriding of the head and the staff. In some schools staff as a whole or via some representative group are plainly involved in both the formulation of policy and/or decisions about proposed alternative courses of action, eg over matters such as the pattern of timings for the school day or changes in the school/college's overall curriculum. In other places such staff participation as exists may be seen to be no more than an opportunity to discuss things before someone else – the head, the senior team, the governors – decides what direction the school should follow.

I have tried to present these various scenarios dispassionately. All they are intended to help me underscore is the need here to look behind the form adopted by any school/college to describe the ways in which responsibility for the school's destiny is distributed and exercised. To answer this second part of the question adequately you must in your own school/college situation distil, openly and honestly, the reality of whose views and opinions routinely influence the direction the school is to follow and what the different degrees of that influence may be.

Question 3. Who are our customers?

The response here is normally defined more easily. Pupils and their parents (as individuals, not as a collective) must come first in any school or college list. However, most schools/colleges these days have other groups of regular users, such as:

- those who hire the premises;
- community groups who use facilities free of charge because of the nature of their activity and the college's support for it;
- groups whom the school invites to attend various school functions such as plays or concerts.

However, having defined my use of the word customer in very broad terms at the start of the previous chapter, I must caution against an over-literal interpretation on those lines here. In one sense anyone on whom the school has any impact at all through its various manifestations is a customer. In this sense any visitor to the school is a customer, as are its neighbours (as described earlier). In practice this is an effective way to regard such groups and the school's responsibility to each and every one of such groups can be discerned by utilising the definition I used in Chapter 4.

However, at this point it is not necessary to list *every* such group by name. What is required is:

(a)   a list of the core customers – those groups or persons whom the school/college sees as its prime concern: almost invariably those towards whom the school's/college's core purpose is deliberately directed;

(b)   any other groups the school wishes to add to the core list, usually in order to extend its area of operation either in principle (eg by adding adult students to the target groups of core customers because the school/college is consciously moving to 'community college' status) or for the pragmatic reason of enlarging the school's resources in order to meet its core purpose more effectively; this obviously occurs when a school/college decides to let its facilities more aggressively and for more extended periods;

(c)   any other group(s) whose interest in the school/college it *wishes* to take into consideration in defining/refining its objectives such as the visitors and local residents referred to above; one can tell on entering any school whether it regards visitors as customers in the Deming sense or whether it sees them (as sadly many still do) as inevitable but unwanted interferers!

Question 4. *What do each of these customers want from us?*

It is very probable that in delineating your response to the previous question you will feel that you have implicitly answered this one. Nevertheless it is a crucial step in this approach now to take each group of customers in the list emerging from Question 3 and write their basic expectations against each.

Once again at this stage be as precise as you can, but not too detailed. That is what I mean by 'basic' in the sentence above. It is obviously impractical to try to spell out in every detail the expectation of each parent for their individual child. It is also easy to fall into the trap of cynicism and describe here what we all know every parent would *like:* a GNVQ Advanced with distinction or 3 Grade 'A' A-levels for their son or daughter.

Attempt only to summarise the key demands, the end objectives of your school/college process, which you believe each group of your customers is implicitly making. Unless you can capture this 'customers'-eye' view of their end objectives for the school with some accuracy the value of this whole approach will be diminished. As another enthusiast for the potential value for schools/colleges in Deming's ideas said of this aspect of his work: 'It offers us the chance to view ourselves from the customer's eye – to understand what the school… looks like to children growing up today' (Rhodes, 1990).

There follows an illustration of meeting customer expectations in practice.

In the early days of one community school's development from an existing comprehensive one of its most successful evening classes was yoga. Without knowing very much about this subject, discussions with the teacher convinced me that one of the main reasons for her success in regularly recruiting and retaining such a large group was her ability to strike the correct balance between the physical and more meditative aspects of the activity. In order to achieve this she needed to be able to bring her class to a close on some occasions less abruptly than the formal 9 pm ending of all the other groups and classes being run that evening.

Because of the school's infancy in its community work at this stage its time schedules for the caretaking team had been worked out on the assumption that the latest any individual evening group member would leave the building would be 9.15 pm. This assumption proved to be occasionally inaccurate in the case of the yoga group. Anyone versed in school/college life will know the next part of this saga without my needing to go into too many details. The building caretaker, normally a reasonably relaxed person, became very agitated and began to invoke the letter of the procedures by which the extended evening activities had been established, saying that it was wrong for one set of users to enjoy privileges that others didn't and that if the line on finishing times was not held, 'Where it would all end nobody could guess' etc.

The problem was solved by the senior caretaker who had, I believe, an uncanny instinct for the concept of 'customer expectation' I am attempting to illustrate here. He explained to the building caretaker the basis on which the school was trying to extend its services to a wider community, saying that in so doing it was raising its own profile and reputation amongst that community and, where possible, also raising some extra revenue. On all three of these counts he explained that the yoga group were a new but very important group of people who had slightly different needs to those in other groups, and for whom the school had to provide a slightly different kind of service (the difference between 9.15 pm and 9.30 pm on one evening a week three or four times a term). He then asked the building caretaker to propose his own solution to the practical difficulty this greater flexibility posed for him and offered his help with adjusting the present arrangements. The solution was not produced instantly, but the yoga teacher never had reason to complain again about an interrupted and rushed finish to her class, and on subsequent occasions the building caretaker could be heard explaining the need for certain amendments to cleaning routines in similar terms to members of his cleaning team. The issue was resolved, I believe, because the senior caretaker took seriously the expectations of the school's new customers, and gave life to them.

Question 5. What resources do we have with which to do these things?

All that is required here is a realistic summary of the total amount of each of the major categories of resource at the school's/college's disposal as listed in the linear version of this model in Chapter 4.

The issues of alternative, strategically different ways of deploying those resources are best considered after the strategic review promoted by this approach has been completed.

The question of resources is needed here only to put into the strategic equation the unavoidable constraints on objectives which are placed by the current maxima of resource in each category.

Question 6. What do we want our school to do?

It is at this point, and only now, that this approach invites you to bring to bear upon your school's/college's situation your own perceptions of the best courses of action to be followed in order to meet your core purpose.

In most schools and colleges the most critical choices are those which go into defining the curriculum, the range of subjects and skills to be taught and the weighting accorded to each by the total amount of teaching time devoted to them. To a large extent, even post-Dearing, for schools teaching the pre-16 age groups only (Key Stages 1–4) this choice is now determined by law in the form of the National Curriculum. Nevertheless, even in these schools areas of significant choice about curriculum do remain, especially at Key Stage 4. Beyond 16, though NVQs and GNVQs appear to be moving the whole system to a more uniform structure, in effect very large elements of choice still pertain.

Outside the curriculum itself all schools and colleges still have to exercise choice between alternatives in order to meet their purposes. What this question requires therefore is a clear listing of the alternatives for each of the major areas of school/college activity preferred by those listed in response to Question 2 (the school's 'owners'), in the sense of those who in reality determine the way it operates, and therefore those whose preferences will determine its policies.

Once again the response needed here is at the broad but fundamental level required at several points earlier. The areas of activity which most determine the shape of the school's response are:

- the school/college curriculum;
- the school's/college's policy on teaching and learning (which determines how the curriculum will be delivered, including its explicit approach to assessment, recording and reporting);
- the structure of the school day/week/term;

- the age, experience, qualifications and enthusiasm of its staff (teaching and non-teaching);
- the deployment of these staff (timetables, workloads, expectations);
- the management structure chosen by the school (including the role of governors and any other partners in overseeing the school/college).

In each of these activity areas there are always significant, broad policy-level choices to be made. To exemplify with just one instance: both the crucial decision of the loading factor of teaching to non-teaching time chosen by a secondary school and the size of teaching groups it wishes to utilise in the different ages/Key Stages combine to influence the quality of the learning experience of the individual pupil. Very large teaching groups are not seen as desirable by the teaching profession in general and by secondary subject specialists in particular. However, heavy loads of teaching (and the marking which they produce) are not welcome either. These two factors are in effect in tension with each other – the more teaching periods a school timetabler can deploy the greater number of teaching groups can be taught and therefore the smaller the average size of those groups. However the price paid for that option is an increased overall teaching load, one outcome of which may well be a more weary and therefore probably less inventive and imaginative teaching force.

Setting out the preferences (and prejudices) which the key policy makers in any school/college bring to such choices is essential if strategy is to be reviewed and developed effectively by this method.

Question 7. Which of our customers' 'wishes' will be met by our desired courses of action?

This is the crucial check-list question, which draws out the degree of match between the end objectives of the school's various customer groups and the school's own preferred objectives. It is possibly better addressed in the form, 'To what extent do our preferred objectives or courses of action meet our customers' objectives?' At a first level it facilitates a visual check as to where the school's objectives are meeting each of the main end objectives of its customers and where they are not.

There is, however, a more critical second level, where failure by a school to provide what its key customers want (for instance, a well ordered and safe environment for learning) may lead to a collapse of customer confidence. Any school faced with this situation must consider amending its objectives in order to improve the match between its own objectives and those of its customers.

It is possible also that examination of this checking system may point up potential but, until then, unseen clashes between one set of customer's end objectives and another. The school/college, as we have already considered, then has to make the difficult choice as to which of the conflicting interests it will serve (always assuming that it cannot find a way of meeting both by, once more, adjusting one of its own chosen courses of action).

Conclusion

For those of you who, as I do, like to have a visual way of checking that you have taken each key factor into consideration in a process such as the one described above, I conclude this 'Customer' approach to strategy review and development with a chart which can easily be photocopied and/or adapted to meet your own needs in this regard. All that is required is that you give each of your 'customer end objectives' (your answers to Question 4) and each of 'the school's/college's objectives' (your answers to Question 6) a reference number.

The former are probably better shown as a combination of cardinal numbers relating to each customer group (the first number) followed by a second number relating to each of the objectives that group of customers brings to its expectations of what your school/college will provide: this system is illustrated on the attached chart.

The latter group (the school's own objectives) can then be referenced by, say, a sequence of capital letters. If you find you have more than 26 you have too many for this purpose!

Chart for Cross-referencing Objectives

Customer Objectives [Ref. Nos.]	School/College Objectives [Ref: Letters]									
	A	B	C	D	E	F	G	H	J	K
1. 1										
1. 2										
1. 3. 1										
1. 3. 2										
2. 1										
2. 2										
2. 3. 1										
2. 3. 2										
3. 1										
3. 2										
3. 3. 1										
3. 3. 2										
4. 1										
4. 2										
4. 3. 1										
4. 3. 2										

6

Competencies and Standards: Other Useful Frameworks for Strategic Review and Development

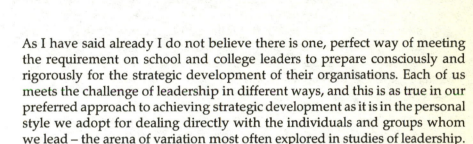

As I have said already I do not believe there is one, perfect way of meeting the requirement on school and college leaders to prepare consciously and rigorously for the strategic development of their organisations. Each of us meets the challenge of leadership in different ways, and this is as true in our preferred approach to achieving strategic development as it is in the personal style we adopt for dealing directly with the individuals and groups whom we lead – the arena of variation most often explored in studies of leadership.

I have also made clear my belief that, however we devise our strategic development plan for our school/college, the process involves a *reframing* of the existing set of perceptions, beliefs, values and purposes which we hold about our organisation. The two approaches proposed so far both start from that premise and offer structures which attempt to force us to construct our strategy from a reconsideration of organisational fundamentals

Others may not find these approaches as appealing or helpful as I did. The option of the most apposite framework – the one which best suits your own sense of your needs – will be better made therefore if the repertoire of choice is wider; and wider in terms of the type of frameworks provided and the concepts on which these are built rather than wider simply meaning more numerous. To this end this chapter presents three more possible ways of tackling the essential task of reframing, all of which start from a completely different conceptual point to the two approaches considered thus far. Their common starting point is that they are derived from either a functional analysis of school leadership or from a combination of that and analysis of the associated personal qualities required of those who exercise that leadership. The resulting elements of these analyses are what are now known, largely as a result of the jargon enshrined by the work of the National Council for Vocational Qualifications (NCVQ), as competencies or standards. They also contrast with the first two approaches in that they have been devised entirely from thinking/development carried out within educational contexts, albeit using patterns of thought and procedures of analysis first used with managers and leaders in other, mainly business, contexts. The three frameworks are:

- the Standards for School Management (1992);
- the Headteachers' Leadership and Management Programme (HEAD-LAMP) Tasks and Abilities (1995);
- the National Professional Qualification for Headship (1996).

Standards for School Management

These were the result of a pilot project undertaken by School Management South (SMS), a consortium of 14 LEAs in the south east of England, with support from the Employment Department. The standards were derived, as required by the Employment Department's national standards programme, by means of a series of functional analysis workshops designed to distil the competencies (or standards) required to manage a school effectively.

As a process, the functional analysis of any area of occupation requires the identification and definition of the following:

(a) a key purpose   (d) elements of competence
(b) key roles   (e) performance criteria
(c) units of competence   (f) range statements.

The objective behind this 'functional analysis' procedure is the laudable one of attempting to define with precision the various processes people need to be able to carry out effectively if they are to be wholly competent in the task or function they are undertaking. The procedure was first devised for use with programmes for YTS trainees in the 1980s. It still provides the conceptual basis for the work of the NCVQ.

The functional map

For our purpose however we need only be concerned with the first three or four of the stages listed. This is because our interest lies in the use of the outcomes as a functional map (or framework) against which a school/college may usefully revisit its current management practice and by that means reappraise its whole strategic direction. We are not concerned with the application of the competencies to the performance of individual managers. The basic map is reproduced as Figure 6.1.

However, in case some readers find the next layer of detail helpful for their own strategic review and development purposes, I also include (Figure 6.2) the 'elements of competence' which comprise each of the units of competence shown in Figure 6.1.

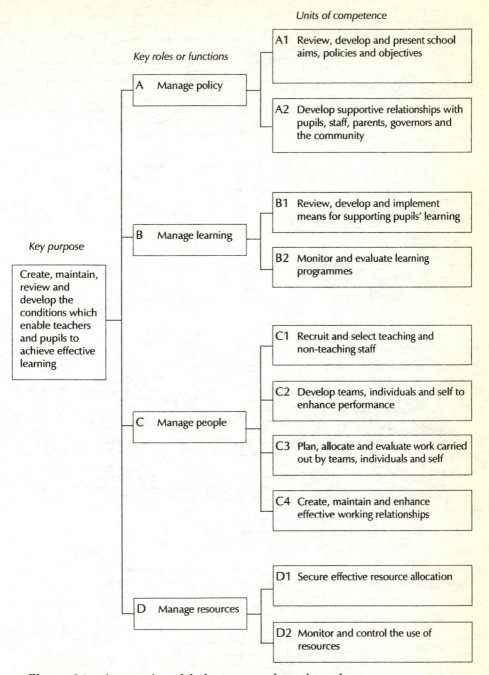

Figure 6.1   *An overview of the key purpose, key roles and units of competence for school management*

| A1 | Review, develop and present school aims, policies and objectives | A1.1 Identify opportunities and constraints on aims, policies and objectives
A1.2 Encourage discussion of school aims, policies and objectives
A1.3 Develop school aims, policies and objectives
A1.4 Seek agreement and disseminate school aims, policies and objectives
A1.5 Evaluate and review effectiveness of school aims, policies and objectives |

| A2 | Develop supportive relationships with pupils, staff, parents, governors and the community | A2.1 Identify problems and opportunities
A2.2 Develop and maintain positive relationships with interested parties
A2.3 Promote the school and its services
A2.4 Recruit pupils and operate admissions policy
A2.5 Evaluate and review relationships and promotion of school |

| B1 | Review, develop and implement means for supporting pupils' learning | B1.1 Identify learning needs of individuals and groups of pupils
B1.2 Review, develop and agree means of planning and supporting learning
B1.3 Implement learning programmes |

| B2 | Monitor and evaluate learning programmes | B2.1 Monitor delivery of learning programmes
B2.2 Evaluate effectiveness of learning programmes |

| C1 | Recruit and select teaching and non-teaching staff | C1.1 Define future personnel requirements
C1.2 Determine recruitment methods
C1.3 Determine specifications to secure quality people
C1.4 Assess and select candidates against team and school requirements |

| C2 | Develop teams, individuals and self to enhance performance | C2.1 Develop and improve teams through planning and activities
C2.2 Identify, review and improve development activities for individuals
C2.3 Develop oneself within the job role
C2.4 Evaluate and improve the development processes used |

| C3 | Plan, allocate and evaluate work carried out by teams, individuals and self | C3.1 Set and update work objectives for teams and individuals
C3.2 Plan activities and determine work methods to achieve objectives
C3.3 Negotiate work allocation and evaluate teams, individuals and self against objectives
C3.4 Provide feedback to teams and individuals on their performance |

| C4 | Create, maintain and enhance effective working relationships | C4.1 Establish and maintain the trust and support of one's staff
C4.2 Establish and maintain the trust and support of one's immediate manager
C4.3 Establish and maintain relationships with colleagues
C4.4 Identify and minimise interpersonal conflict
C4.5 Implement disciplinary and grievance procedures
C4.6 Counsel staff |

| D1 | Secure effective resource allocation | D1.1 Identify resources necessary to support learning
D1.2 Develop and maintain means of generating income and resources
D1.3 Justify proposals for expenditure
D1.4 Negotiate and agree budgets
D1.5 Establish and maintain supply of resources |

| D2 | Monitor and control the use of resources | D2.1 Control costs and enhance value
D2.2 Monitor and control activities against budgets
D2.3 Create and maintain the necessary environment for effective learning |

Figure 6.2   *Units and elements of competence*

Using the Functional Map for Strategic Development

When the SMS standards were being tested in schools to ascertain both their validity as an analytical model and their usefulness, one of the most frequent reactions related to their value as a tool for in-depth review of the school's fundamental structures and purposes. Although this was not the objective for which they had been created, Peter Earley and his team found that several schools reported on the benefits they had derived from this use of the standards. Because it was not the main focus of the pilot, direct, factual and quantitative evidence on how this particular effect was achieved was not easily acquired. However, the anecdotal evidence led me to conclude that the best way to use the standards for this purpose was as follows.

Step 1

The senior team is introduced to the functional map of the management of a school/college provided by the SMS standards and takes away a copy to study. Following this they meet to discuss their several understandings of the functional map. This meeting leads quickly to a process I call discussion by example: members of the team explain their understanding of the various parts of the analysis by exemplifying certain of the 'elements' of competence through reference to the individual colleague (eg senior teacher in charge of administration) or group of colleagues (eg heads of department/subject co-ordinators) who currently have responsibility for those tasks in the school.

What then begins to emerge is that in some instances several people are identified by different members of the senior team as being primarily responsible for ensuring the completion of one particular task or function, while in the case of other tasks no one seems to have overall charge (although several people seemed to contribute towards their completion). Rather than let any of these debates on detail develop, this initial discussion should be kept moving so that all areas of the map are briefly reviewed. Then as soon as everyone is sure they understand the basic 'mechanics' of the functional map – the relationship between the key purpose and the key roles, the links between each of those roles and the associated units of competence and their connection to the various elements – move to Step 2.

Step 2

Each member of the team now takes away an extended copy of the units and elements, which provides space for written comment to the right (A3 size paper with Figure 6.2 reproduced on the left meets the purpose). Working alone everyone writes in against each unit of competence and against each element the name of the colleague who they think currently holds *the responsibility for ensuring* that that particular aspect of the school's management is carried out effectively. Note the italics. In some instances the colleague whose name is recorded will actually carry out the tasks (or parts of them) implicit in the particular unit or element. In other cases the tasks implied (or the bulk of them) will actually be carried out by others. What is sought here is the name of the person who is *responsible* for seeing that part of the overall functioning of the school/college actually takes place, and to good effect.

This exercise should not be forced. If anyone is uncertain which of two (or more) colleagues holds a particular responsibility both (all) names should be recorded. If the doubt is that the respondent cannot think of anyone who is responsible for a certain unit or element no name should be recorded. It is most important to the potential success of this review that these guidelines are followed.

Step 3
One member of the team accepts the task of collating all the individual responses on to a single set of sheets, with each entry annotated with the initials of the team member who has provided the information.This is then given to all team members in preparation for a further meeting, at which the outcomes can be reviewed and the resulting conclusions considered in terms of the insights they provoke of the school's/college's current ways of conducting its affairs and the implications of these for its further, strategic development.

Step 4
In the discussion of the findings of this 'who is responsible for what' exercise three related scenarios usually emerge.

1. In all but the smallest schools, where it is inevitable that the head's name will be recorded against every element (and where therefore this particular approach is not advisable), some elements will not be recorded as being anyone's prime responsibility, eg C2.4.
2. Some elements will appear to be the responsibility of almost everyone, or at least of a significant proportion of the senior team. C4.3 is a possible example of this.

   Note, however, that one element – C2.3 – *is* everyone's responsibility With the benefit of hindsight it seems to me to be an odd one to include in an analysis which purports to map school management as a whole.
3. Team members will be sure other elements are being covered by someone, but no one will have clearly identified who that someone is, eg D2.1.

This pattern of triple scenarios can be further clarified. Elements where someone is clearly seen to be doing something, but no one actually appears to exercise overall routine responsibility for its direction, tend to fall most frequently in the 'monitor and evaluate' categories. The prime example of this is B2.2, where the overall responsibility for the process of evaluating the effectiveness of learning is rarely located specifically with any one person.

Almost as much concern is usually raised by the discovery that several elements of the 'Manage people' role are claimed by everyone (or most people) on the senior team but with no one, or only the head, recognised as the manager of a whole unit: that particular response occurs most frequently in the case of unit C4. In any area of management the danger inherent in everyone saying something is part of their responsibility and no one accepting that it is their job to see that it is done is famously expressed by Murphy in one of his laws: 'If it's everybody's responsibility nobody does it.'

The usual conclusion from the third scenario is that these elements are left to chance. They are functions which are met whenever someone remembers, and has time to do them. If no one remembers they do not get done.

Step 5

In order to examine why these various omissions occur it is necessary now to move *backwards* through the model to examine the team's understanding of each of the key roles and to establish who, if anyone, accepts the overall responsibility for each role.

Except in the very rare circumstance where it is found that no one currently occupies one or other of the four roles, at this stage it is often the head who claims responsibility for the oversight. Whether it is the head or another team member (or members) who claim any particular role, the same question should be asked next, 'Exactly how, routinely, is this responsibility exercised?' What *active steps* does this person regularly take in order to ensure that the function is fulfilled? Very often the team will conclude that the honest response to this question is a negative one; that fulfilment of this role normally happens only when an error occurs or an omission is revealed and a member of the senior team is called upon to deal with it.

An example of this to which I was a party many years ago arose over the question of homework. A school which was being criticised by its parents for not making as much use of homework as parents expected decided to do something to meet this criticism. Following a staff meeting on the matter each department put forward a revised specification of its homework require- ments for each year group. A working group reviewed each of these, re- quested a decrease in one or two of the requests and an increase in one area and then drew up the new homework timetable. This was sent to all depart- ments for final comment before being sent to parents with a covering letter from the head. In this he acknowledged the rectitude of much of the criticism and presented the brave new world in the form of the new homework timetable and its accompanying notes on the loads expected of individual pupils in different years and of differing abilities. This action met with

virtually 100 per cent approbation from parents and the school settled down
to enjoy its renewed popularity.

Some months later, however, one of the school's most active parent
supporters – chair of her children's house PTA and vice-chair of the school's
central PTA – met the head at a school function and enquired how the new
homework 'policy' was working out. The head remarked on how well it had
gone down with parents and said that the staff too had clearly benefited from
facing up to the issue of homework as a whole staff. Considering the part
played by homework in the learning process and reviewing the demands
made on pupils by all the departments had refocused staff attention on the
importance of homework. The parent then told the head that none of her
three children (in the terminology of today's world she had one in Year 13,
another in Year 10 and a third in Year 8) had had any homework (other than
bits of the 'Finish off work started in class' variety) set for almost a month. I
will not continue this anecdote further in itself, since further details are
unnecessary to my purpose in telling it. It is sufficient to note here that my
confidence in this part of our school's operation and in our capability as a
management team was, if not shattered, severely dented!

Rapid investigation confirmed the facts and revealed a perfect example of
the situation concerning the exercise of management responsibilities described above. All of us in the management team acknowledged that we all
shared a responsibility to 'Manage learning' (key role B) and therefore to
'Monitor and evaluate learning programmes' (unit B2). We established that
the deputy head (curriculum) accepted prime responsibility for this role,
though my personal intervention over the initial issue of loss of parental
confidence in our previous homework policy had almost certainly confused
things. However our most important learning came when we asked the
question about *who had actually done anything* to carry out element B2.1 –
'Monitor delivery of learning programmes' – in relation to this particular
aspect of our responsibilities. The answer of course was no one, at least until
it had been pointed out to us that something we all believed was happening
was not. In other words we discovered that we only exercised this kind of
responsibilty reactively. More importantly we then had to ask *why* this was
so.

The answer was not easy to discern. The very fact that this sin of omission
has been committed means that in any case of this kind we are being driven
more by our assumptions about the situation than by any conscious analysis
of it. We finally decided that we had let our assumptions lead us to the
conclusion that, having discussed both the need for a revised approach to
homework and the type of response we should make to this need, it was not
necessary to *do anything*. This assumption was of course underpinned by a
whole host of others – in particular about the nature of professional relationships within departments (as well as in the school at large) and about precisely

how these should be managed, and about the real (ie educational) value of homework as compared to its importance in the eyes of most parents. This was an issue not explored earlier in our reactive response to parental criticism. Thus inexorably we were forced back towards an examination of our own interpretation of our purposes as a school, and in particular of the ways in which the routine exercise of our responsibilities so significantly shaped and reshaped (distorted?) these.

In this way the process of reappraisal, by starting from a close examination of current management practice in the school/college, can lead to the kind of practical re-examination of fundamentals necessary to enable real strategic development to begin.

Conclusions on this use of the SMS model

This model has provided a useful tool of strategic development for those schools which naturally incline towards a starting point located in the analysis of 'the here and now of the who does what'.

Unlike some other audit systems its conceptual basis in the functional analysis of workplace competencies seems to lead some schools to a fundamental review of purpose, the impact on that of changing circumstances and the reflection of those in terms of possible alternative practice. I find it impossible to explain why this should be so. Maybe it was simply that this form of analysis reached schools during a period when the basic assumptions about the nature of schooling were being questioned to such an extent that the unspoken consensus about the purpose and nature of education which was present in earlier times (the 1960s especially) has been lost. For many schools this may have generated the feeling that at this stage in their development this approach to their strategic growth seemed especially congruent with the present times.

The two remaining frameworks presented in this chapter, though owing something to the current vogue for analyses deriving from the idea of competencies, both focus specifically on the role of the headteacher. They may therefore appear usable only by individuals who hold or aspire to this role. I am certain that they can provide a basis for useful analysis by either the senior team or a team with wider staff representation put together for the purpose of conducting a strategic review of the school/college. By focusing on the specific tasks of the head/principal and the knowledge and abilities required to carry out those tasks they promote a wholesale examination of the school's/college's activities. First, because it arrived on the scene first and is therefore in a more developed state, the Headteachers' Leadership and Management Programme (HEADLAMP) framework.

HEADLAMP

This programme is set out in the form of a list of

- six areas of leadership and management tasks; and
- eight types of leadership and management abilities.

These were devised by the Teacher Training Agency (TTA) in 1995 as a specific 'initiative to support newly appointed headteachers'. Heads appointed to maintained schools (primary or secondary) receive up to £2,500 worth of support for their own personal development plan at any time within the first two years of taking up their appointment. In order to qualify for this support the training must focus on one or more of the 'tasks and abilities' defined by the TTA as central to the delivery of effective leadership and management by headteachers.

Figure 6.3 sets out these tasks and abilities as presented by the TTA in their 'Procedures' document in the summer of 1995.

Using the HEADLAMP framework

As with the use of the Standards of School Management model, by taking each of these tasks and abilities in turn and setting them along side the existing school situation one can create a potential framework for the fundamental review of the school's strategic position. Except that in this instance, instead of beginning with the question, 'Who does that now?' which was the starting point for schools using the SSM model, I recommend an interrogation of the framework which starts by asking 'What?' or 'How?' of each aspect of this framework. This is the basis for the proforma which follows. As on previous occasions my strong recommendation is that you use it as it is, until your own familiarity with the probing it is designed to promote leads you instinctively to raise your own, better questions of your current and future situations.

On the following pages you will find each of the tasks and abilities listed in Figure 6.3 set out in the left-hand columns. Against each of them I have posed a series of 'Interrogatives', questions to prompt the probing of your current and possible future situations needed to shape your strategic plan.

The remaining two columns relate respectively to your response to the prompts in terms of your present situation (the 'Now' column) and 'In the light of possible futures'. I suggest that, if you decide to use this particular framework, you experiment with the obvious alternatives of either completing all the 'Now' responses first before proceeding to respond again in relation to the future, or responding to each of the various tasks and abilities in turn in terms of both present and possible future conditions. Whichever option you choose you will clearly need more space for your responses than it is possible to provide here.

HEADLAMP Leadership and Management Tasks and Abilities

Each headteacher's training programme will need to focus on one or more of a range of leadership and management tasks aimed at promoting high standards and effective teaching and learning in the school, drawn from the following:

1. defining the aims and objectives of the school;
2. developing, implementing, monitoring and reviewing policies for all aspects of the school, including the curriculum, assessment, classroom organisation and management, teaching approaches and pupil support;
3. planning and managing resource provision;
4. assessing and reviewing standards of pupils' achievements and the quality of teaching and learning;
5. selecting and managing staff, and appraising their performance and development needs;
6. liaising with parents, the local community and other organisations and institutions.

In addition, and in relation to the selected tasks, each headteacher's training programme will need to focus on one or more of a range of leadership and management abilities, including the ability to:

1. give a clear sense of direction and purpose in order to achieve the school's mission and inspire staff and pupils alike;
2. anticipate problems, make judgements and take decisions;
3. adapt to changing circumstances and new ideas;
4. solve problems;
5. negotiate, delegate, consult and coordinate the efforts of others;
6. follow through and pursue policies to implementation and monitor and review their effectiveness in practice;
7. understand and keep up to date with current educational and management issues and identify their relevance to the school;
8. communicate effectively with staff at all levels, pupils, parents, governors and the wider community.

Each headteacher's training programme should set these tasks and abilities into the broader context of leadership, ie setting the tone and style of the school, developing its ethos, generating the spirit and purpose of the school, and conveying this to pupils, staff, parents and the wider community.

Figure 6.3 *HEADLAMP leadership and management tasks and abilities*

Figure 6.4 *HEADLAMP framework for strategic review and development*

	Task area	Interrogatives	Strategic responses		
			Now		**In the light of possible futures?**
T1	Defining the aims and objectives of the school	What is this school's principal aim? What are the key objectives by which this aim will be realised? (six maximum, to limit 'the catch-all' tendency)			
T2	Developing, implementing, monitoring and reviewing policies – for all aspects of the school – including the curriculum, assessment, classroom organisation and management, teaching approaches and pupil support	For each of the following respond to the question. *How do/should we in the future* ■ develop [D]? ■ implement? [I] ■ monitor and review [M]? CURRICULUM [D] [I] [M] ASSESSMENT [D] [I] [M] CLASSROOM O and M [D] [I] [M]			

Figure 6.4 *(continued) HEADLAMP framework for strategic review and development*

Task area	Interrogatives	Strategic responses		
			Now	In the light of possible futures?
	TEACHING APPROACHES	[D] [I] [M]		
	PUPIL SUPPORT	[D] [I] [M]		
T3 Planning and managing resource provision	What procedures does the school use to *plan* the deployment of its resources? How are resources *managed* (directed and monitored) in the school?			
T4 Assessing and reviewing standards of pupils' achievements and the quality of teaching and learning	What is the school's assessment policy? How does it relate to or inform the teaching and learning process? How does the school review the standards achieved by its pupils? Against what criteria?			
T2				

	How is the quality of teaching and learning monitored? How routine are these procedures?		
T5	Selecting and managing staff, and appraising their performance	What procedures are in place for the recruitment staff? How effective do these appear to be? What are the principles behind the school's management structures? Are these congruent with the school's aims and objectives? How are staff appraised? What impact does staff appraisal have on school development?	
T6	Liaising with parents, the local community and other organisations and institutions	How does the school maintain effective (two-way) contacts with parents – as individuals and as a representative group?	

Figure 6.4 *HEADLAMP framework for strategic review and development*

Task area	Interrogatives	Strategic responses	
		Now	In the light of possible futures?
	What does your school mean by the phrase 'the local community' (which people or groups are included and which are not)?		
	How does the school keep itself in touch with its local community?		
	With what other organisations and institutions does the school have to maintain effective contact?		
	How does it do this?		
	How is the whole area of 'external communication' kept under regular review?		

Abilities	Interrogatives	Now	In the light of possible futures
A1	Give a clear sense of direction and purpose in order to achieve the school's mission and inspire staff and pupils alike	Can all members of staff explain clearly (to visitors) what the school is seeking to achieve (its mission)?		
		What is the evidence that staff are inspired (excited?) by the school's mission?		

	How *enthusiastic* are pupils about the school and their place in it?		
A2	Anticipate problems, make judgements and take decisions	What are the main problems facing the school at present? (Maximum of five suggested to force prioritisation)	
		What options are open to the school to deal with each of these problems and what criteria might be used to choose between them?	Option Criteria Option Criteria Option Criteria Option Criteria Option Criteria
		How will the decision on a chosen course of action be reached?	
A3	Adapt to changing circumstances and new ideas	What 'changing circumstances' face the school at present? (Maximum of five recommended)	
		What significant new ideas are currently circulating/have circulated recently? (No more than three recommended)	

Figure 6.4 *HEADLAMP framework for strategic review and development*

Abilities	Interrogatives	Now	In the light of possible futures?
	What procedures does the school have in place to deal with changes thrust upon it or proposed?		
	How are ideas disseminated in the school?		
A4 Solve problems	What kinds of whole-school problems (eg levels of motivation for work in Year 10) is the school facing at present? (Again – maximum of five recommended)		
	What systems does the school deploy to respond to whole-school problems as they occur?		
	How effective are they?		

A5	Negotiate, delegate, consult and coordinate the efforts of others	For each of the four processes listed in this ability – negotiate (N), delegate (D), consult (CT), coordinate (CO) – give one recent example of the school's way of providing for this and, in the 'futures' column, say whether you believe the school's systems to be adequate for this particular purpose (and why or why not). N D CT CO	
A6	Follow through and pursue policies to implementation and monitor and review their effectiveness in practice	What are the school's systems for action planning – for identifying who should do what by when and to what 'success criteria'? How does the school check that it has carried out its intentions? How does the school keep the effectiveness of its practices under regular review?	
A7	Understand and keep up to date with current educational and management issues and identify their relevance to the school	What recent evidence is there that the school is keeping itself up to date educationally? When were the management structures and responsibilities last compared formally with the latest thinking about the management of organisations? What was concluded?	

Figure 6.4 *HEADLAMP framework for strategic review and development*

	Abilities	Interrogatives	Now	In the light of possible futures?
		How does the school discriminate between the valuable and the vogue?		
A8	Communicate effectively with staff – at all levels – pupils, parents, governors and the wider community	For each of these groups review briefly the systems used by the school for oral communication (OC) and for communication in print (CP) in the 'Now' column		
		In the 'futures' column consider possible alternatives in the light of future needs/current dissatisfaction		
		▪ teaching staff (TS)	TS/OC CP	
		▪ non-teaching staff (NTS)	NTS/OC CP	
		▪ pupils (P)	P/OC CP	

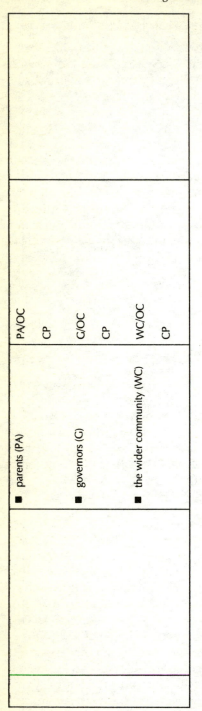

- parents (PA)   PA/OC
                                      CP

- governors (G)   G/OC
                                      CP

- the wider community (WC)   WC/OC
                                      CP

Figure 6.4   *HEADLAMP framework for strategic review and development*

National Professional Qualification for Headship

I include this third framework here mainly for the sake of completeness. It has much in common with the HEADLAMP lists of the tasks and abilities central to the effective operation of leadership and management in schools/ colleges. At the time of writing (mid-1996) this new qualification is still in the initial stages of development. It is likely to change significantly in the light of trials (involving aspiring heads and regional providers) designed to test its practicality as a basis both for training and assessment before full implementation from September 1997. Nevertheless it seems appropriate to include it here as an indication of the latest way in which school/college leadership is being defined: a way which may well become the national yardstick for thinking about the direction of schools/colleges for the foreseeable future.

The first stage of consultation revealed the need to devise national standards for headship to 'underpin the qualification'. It is these which provide us with this third and last example of a framework based upon the concept of 'competencies and standards' and offer a further possible basis for the strategic review and development process. Figure 6.5 sets out the draft standards in outline form.

You will see that these are derived conceptually from a combination of the competences approach set out at the beginning of this chapter and the HEADLAMP idea of a discrete set of essential tasks and abilities. They may therefore be used in conjunction with either of the preceding frameworks as a further (and the most recent) refinement of the nature and shape of school/college management. Given the current stage of their development it is not worth investing them with more detailed attention. Nevertheless – alongside whichever of the two preceding frameworks you are most comfortable with – it should be possible for you to make use of the thrust of those parts of these draft national standards which seem to you to offer a different or additional strategic purchase to your analysis.

Conclusion

This chapter has offered you two-plus-one further frameworks for the possible strategic review and analysis of your school/college based upon the ideas of workplace competence and standards. As I have attempted to make clear, I recommend these as possible alternatives to the two more common Systems Analysis and customer-centred approaches set out in earlier chapters because I am convinced that different keys will unlock the doors to progress with genuinely strategic development for different people. It is important, at least initially, to follow the one which appeals to you most. Even then, once you have understood its basic orientation and feel confident that you can use it to explore the fundamental convictions and assumptions which shape your school and its ways of doing things be prepared, as I have repeatedly suggested, to make your own further adaptations. That is what I have found has been most effective in my own experience of using these frameworks to help other schools/colleges develop their strategies for the future.

However, many may not find even these particular alternative approaches to the development of strategy to their taste. I therefore return in the remaining chapters to other forms of strategic review and development based in each case on analyses of schools/colleges as whole organisations.

The basic framework consists of four parts.

1. The core purpose of headship.
2. Five key areas for development and assessment.
3. The leadership and management skills and abilities (needed to meet each of these areas of development and to achieve the core purpose).
4. The underpinning knowledge and understanding required.

The core purpose of headship is described as:

- to provide professional leadership and direction for the continuous improvement of the school.

The five key areas are:

- strategic direction and development of the school;
- learning and teaching in the school;
- people and relationships;
- the deployment and development of human and material resources;
- rendering account of the schools efficiency and effectiveness.

Each of these areas is further subdivided into a series of discrete functions, totalling (at present) 21 in all.

There are 13 *skills and abilities*, which include all those found in the HEADLAMP framework and some notable additions, such as:

- recognise and manage stress in self and others;
- resolve conflicts and deal with aggression;
- understand and interpret statistics and data.

There are seven *areas of knowledge and understanding.*

1. Learning and teaching – curriculum and assessment including the National Curriculum.
2. Strategy and leadership – including development planning.
3. Management.
4. Finance.
5. Human resource management.
6. Legal framework – including the Education Reform Act, Ofsted, the National Curriculum and assessment issues.
7. Governance.

Figure 6.5 *Draft national standards for headship*

7

Continual Transformation: A Learning Organisation's Planned Approach to Strategic Development

Introduction to the Concepts

Henry Mintzberg has been described as 'Canada's best-known guru of management' (Foster, 1989). This followed a speech to members of the Strategic Planning Society in London, where the main thrust of his address, was that the true purposes of strategic planning are frequently misunderstood, particularly by those in business organisations who use the process of strategic planning professionally. He was in fact attacking the basic assumption that all organisations develop best if they proceed along paths determined entirely by rational analysis. The frequent 'buffeting by the wind' that external events often (and internal initiatives sometimes) cause, brings about the inevitable need for adaptations, which in some cases are themselves the immediate source of a further strategy. In other words, to assume that action *always* follows deliberate intention in human affairs is a fallacy.

On the other hand, to assume that nothing is (or can or should be) planned, that all should be left to 'buffeting' by the wind, is equally fallacious. Strategy, claimed Mintzberg, is a combination of both deliberately and thoughtfully chosen intention and response to changing circumstance. He then went on to describe three major schools of thought he had observed in the approach to strategic development:

- the planning school
- the visionary school
- the learning school.

Strict interpreters of the planning school approach strategy work via what I would call a slavish interpretation of the methods we have already met in the early chapters of this book – a strict, almost scientific application of the classic Systems Analysis model.

The visionary approach, according to Foster's article, 'is a semi-conscious process... which takes place in the mind of the leader'. As Foster goes on to say, 'The process may be compared to a hypodermic injection: the active ingredient (the vision) is loaded into a syringe (communication) and injected into [the organisation].' Mintzberg, he says, shows some preference for this approach because it accords most closely with what actually happens in the organisations whose development he has witnessed. My experience teaches me to beware of placing too much reliance on the personal strengths of any one individual as the sole source of a model for others to follow.

The third, learning school, approach occurs when organisations routinely and continuously analyse the outcomes of their own current organisational activities in order to learn from them. Mintzberg characterises this as 'doing something and finding out what works'. Its potential power was born out in the UK by research into 'the learning company' conducted by Mike Pedler *et al.* for the Manpower Services Commission in 1988. Only two of their findings need concern us here.

1. Central to their understanding of a learning organisation is the idea of continuous growth and improvement, but the defining quality they identify is capacity for continual transformation. A learning company, they say, is one that 'facilitates the learning of all its members and continually transforms itself'.

2. They give as one crucial feature of any organisation that seeks to achieve this continual transformation through the learning of all its members the fact that it is always 'open to interrogation from below'. In other words, a learning organisation is one that explicitly and routinely ensures that its systems and structures guarantee that those who define the organisation's policies (and thus determine its present and future strategy), can and do hear the questions raised about its purposes and ways of doing things by those whose task it is to put the strategy into effect.

Putting these specific learning company ideas alongside Mintzberg's three categories of approach to strategic development, it seemed to me possible to provide a framework for strategy development which combined the useful attributes of a planning approach (the structures it offers for one's thinking) with those of the learning approach stressed by Pedler *et al.* (1991): hence the 'learning organisation's planned approach' in this chapter's title. I have also tried to capture something of Mintzberg's preferred visionary approach though not, in this instance, in the form that Mintzberg himself would recognise.

Finally, for the basic format set out below I am indebted to an idea developed in 1990/91 by the National Centre for Innovation (which was established and is run by the National Education Association, the larger of the two teacher associations in the USA) for use with schools which were part of its school renewal network. They believed that in order for schools to be renewed and redeveloped through significant innovation they had to fundamentally reconceptualise the ways in which they went about their work. One method they deployed to help their participating schools do this seemed to me to provide a useful starting point from which schools can 'interrogate' their current ways of doing things in order to try to discover how they might develop them in the future.

Both the actual process of doing this and the cumulative total of the school's/college's findings will enable them to acquire a more strategic view of the school/college as an organisation. By looking at how things work now and comparing these with alternative, preferred future intentions, any organisation will be helped to 'renew' or 'transform' itself. As Mintzberg also observed in his 1989 lecture, 'the structure of an organisation influences its strategic thinking, and vice versa'. What is offered here is a way of examining the current key structures of schools/colleges as organisations against deliberately chosen criteria for their future development.

The remainder of this chapter sets out the process to be followed, but with the two key factors about learning organisations noted above constantly in mind.

1. *The exercise is designed to promote interrogation* – of the basic structures on which your school/college rests and the possible future shape of these. *Note:* The extent to which this interrogation properly meets Pedler's (1988) definition of interrogation from below depends on the means you adopt to conduct the exercise and the use you make of any initial findings from it, as indicated in several of the items in the guidelines below.
2. The *purpose* of the exercise is to move the organisation towards the goal of *continual transformation* through which it will be able to develop its strategy.

Introduction to the Process

Figure 7.1 sets out the basic proforma on which it is recommended that you record your responses to each of the continua in turn. It is probably best to look at this before reading the guidelines below as these refer to the various sections on the proforma.

As with all proforma, be prepared to ignore the restrictions provided by the size of the boxes, writing as little or as much as you wish and using the reverse of the form or other resources as required. Before beginning write in the feature you are considering and the words which define the ends of its continuum.

Figure 7.1

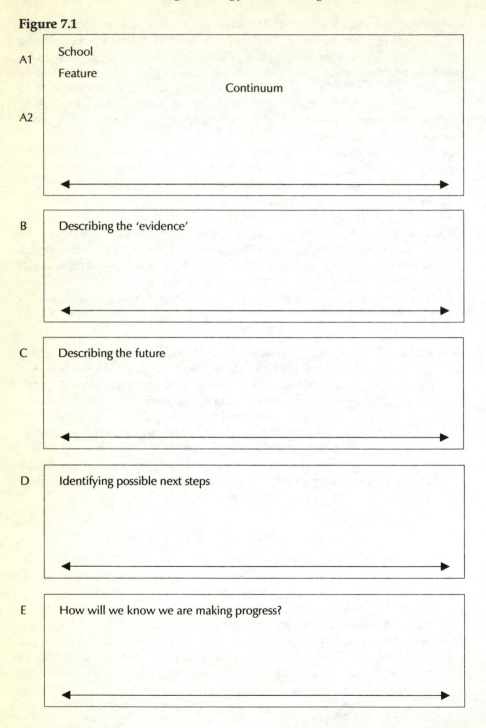

Figure 7.2 *The 12 features and their original continua*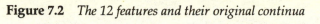

A1 School

Feature

CURRICULUM

Continuum

A2 Dominated by learning and remembering subject content. Skills of flexible learning caught more than taught.

Process dominated; learning to learn, problem solving, interpersonal skills all explicitly taught. Lifelong learning focus within subject discipline framework.

◄───────────────────────────►

A1 School

Feature

TEACHING AND LEARNING

Continuum

A2 Teachers provide source and structure for learning: pupils expected to be good at listening, responding, being patient and on time.

Pupils are active, independent learners who set own goals, find and organise information. Teachers assist in analysis and critical evaluation and provide continuing extra challenge

◄───────────────────────────►

A1 School

Feature

ASSESSMENT

Continuum

A2 Measures performance summatively, largely for purposes of reporting to others (parents etc). Is largely in hands of teachers.

Supports learning; indicates to individual pupils areas of strength and weakness and steps needed for improvement. Is shared by pupils and teachers.

◄───────────────────────────►

Figure 7.2   *continued*

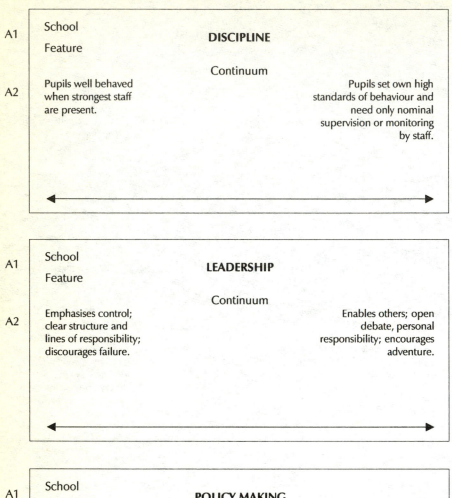

A1   School

Feature

DISCIPLINE

Continuum

A2   Pupils well behaved when strongest staff are present.

Pupils set own high standards of behaviour and need only nominal supervision or monitoring by staff.

A1   School

Feature

LEADERSHIP

Continuum

A2   Emphasises control; clear structure and lines of responsibility; discourages failure.

Enables others; open debate, personal responsibility; encourages adventure.

A1   School

Feature

POLICY MAKING

Continuum

A2   Conceived and determined by school's most senior management.

Arises from consideration by whole staff following consultation with relevant stakeholders.

Figure 7.2   *continued*

A1 | School

Feature

GOVERNANCE AND MANAGEMENT

Continuum

A2 | Formal, top-down
exclusive style.

Collegial task/team
approach, inclusive style.

◄──────────────────────────────────────►

A1 | School

Feature

COMMUNICATION

Continuum

A2 | Characterised by formal
meetings efficiently
conducted. Very effective
in passing information
down the chain.

Open, informal, frequent
contacts between
individuals and groups:
effective in promoting
'interrogation from below'.

◄──────────────────────────────────────►

A1 | School

Feature

STAFF DEVELOPMENT

Continuum

A2 | Provided by external
experts, off site or at
mandatory inset events in
school.

Wide variety of in-school
activity – peer observation,
school-based action
research, changes of role –
supported by selected
specialist training for
individuals or groups.

◄──────────────────────────────────────►

Figure 7.2 *continued*

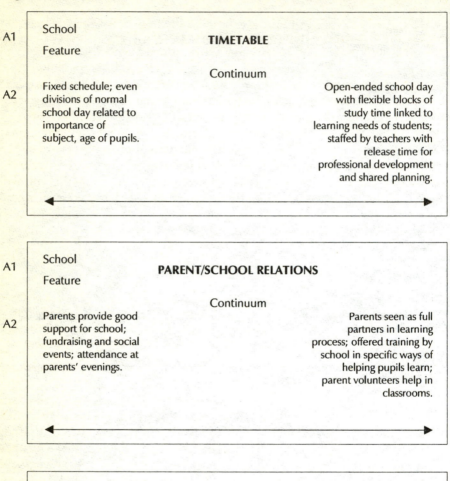

A1   School

Feature

TIMETABLE

Continuum

A2   Fixed schedule; even divisions of normal school day related to importance of subject, age of pupils.

Open-ended school day with flexible blocks of study time linked to learning needs of students; staffed by teachers with release time for professional development and shared planning.

A1   School

Feature

PARENT/SCHOOL RELATIONS

Continuum

A2   Parents provide good support for school; fundraising and social events; attendance at parents' evenings.

Parents seen as full partners in learning process; offered training by school in specific ways of helping pupils learn; parent volunteers help in classrooms.

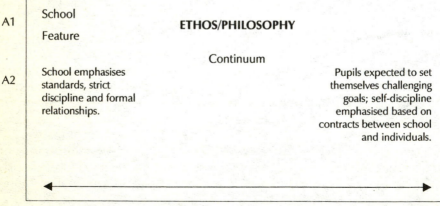

A1   School

Feature

ETHOS/PHILOSOPHY

Continuum

A2   School emphasises standards, strict discipline and formal relationships.

Pupils expected to set themselves challenging goals; self-discipline emphasised based on contracts between school and individuals.

The 12 features [A1]

Set out on the proforma are 12 key, structural features of schools. These are clearly my selection. You may of course decide to use only some of these 12 features, but I would argue that too great a reduction of the total is likely to lead to your garnering too narrow a view of your school for strategic purposes. It is also important to ask yourself if you are not taking out some of the criteria because they are features of your school which you would rather leave untouched. This very decision has, of course, significant strategic implications. If you openly examine these and acknowledge (to yourself) the limitations they impose upon your review of strategy then proceed as you wish.

Alternatively you may wish to add other features of your own or substitute one or more of these for one or some of my original 12. If you do this you will need to create you own definitions for the end points of each of your continua.

The end points of each continuum [A2]

Each continuum carries a set of words at each of its two extremities. The purpose of these is to define:

(a) at the left-hand end – the current situation with regards to that feature in your school;
(b) at the right-hand end – a potential vision of the future state of that feature of your school.

Once again, you may wish to amend these words, in either or both instances, for each continuum in turn. The greatest temptation to do this will be in the case of the left-hand sets of words. As these purport to describe the status quo in your school you may well feel that some correction is needed. My advice here is to avoid making amendments too readily in this instance, as in each case the line represents a continuum between extremes. It is perfectly proper therefore to estimate your school's own current position as lying between the two extremes and to record your evidence for this accordingly (see Describing 'the evidence' below). Only if you are certain that your school's current situation with regard to any feature lies well outside the extreme defined by the words to the left should it be necessary to alter/amend those.

The words to the right may be amended more readily as they describe a desirable possible future state. If you wish to express this in different terminology you should do so, always bearing in mind of course the strategic (ie long-term and significantly altered or improved) purpose of any strategic development.

Once you have decided that you have the necessary continua for your analysis recorded on each of your proforma and have copied in the words defining the left- and right-hand extremities of each, slash the line representing the continuum at the point which best represents your view of where your school is now on that particular dimension of its work.

Note: If you are using this approach with a group of colleagues (the senior team, the governors, all staff etc), it is necessary to decide at this point whether the group arrives at a composite view of where the school currently rests on the particular continuum or whether each individual records their own view (on a separate proforma). Apart from the obvious increase in the amount of paper required there is great advantage in asking each person to record an individual view. This advantage will be clearer at the next stage.

Describing 'the evidence' [B]

What has been 'captured' so far is an impression or perception of the school's current situation with regard to the feature under review.

It is now necessary to record – at B – what aspects of the systems deployed by the school with respect to that feature provide you with your reasons for recording your impression as you have. What evidence – in the form of specific examples of the way the school actually goes about its business in relation to that feature – can you describe here? Who does what? How do they do it? What system is used? What demonstrable effects does that have on pupils, staff, governors, visitors etc? In other words, *how do you know* the school is currently where you say it is on the continuum?

This is where the recording of individual experiences to justify individual perceptions (the positions on the continuum represented by the slashes) by members of a group is especially valuable. When people are asked to describe in some detail the observable reasons they have for forming their judgement of the current situation the subsequent debate is much more likely to lead to a more strategic evaluation of the current situation. The interpretations placed upon the same situation by different people all contribute to the direction an organisation actually follows (as compared to those it may set out intending to follow). Understanding these better is a significant step towards their strategic reappraisal.

The alternative way of proceeding, seeking group agreement to the school's stage of development in relation to each particular feature, leads inevitably to the compromises that traditionally emerge through such an exercise. It also denies the group the opportunity to scrutinise their current practice from the several perspectives provided if everyone not only makes their own assessment but has to justify it by describing the factors which have given rise to it in their own experience.

Describing the future [C]

What is required here is a description of the factors pertaining to the feature under review as they *will be* when the desired state envisioned for the future by the words to the right of the continuum is reached. In terms similar to those used in the previous stage, *how will you know* you have reached the right-hand end of the continuum? This is clearly going to be as a result of a leap of imagination, linked to a more incremental process based upon eradicating or amending those factors in the current situation which need changing.

It is important, however, to record your conclusions here in a style similar to that used at B. You need to write down specific examples of the kinds of systems or behaviours required rather than simply record too generalised a description. One check that this pitfall has been avoided is to compare what you have written with the words at the right-hand end of the continuum above which describe the future state. If this is only or very largely a restatement of those then it is very likely that you need to provide yourself with a more detailed, evidentiary record.

If you are employing this approach using a group the opposite advice applies to that given for individual experiences. Envisioning the future in the light of a detailed review of the present is best done by a group. One idea sparks off another, promoting the very kind of development of strategy that is sought. That is not to say that individuals might not wish to give some quiet thought to their own view of what the future might look like, but the best way to make use of these views is in open debate with others, and it is the group outcome that is best recorded at the end.

Identifying possible next steps [D]

At this point the task is to attempt some definition of what the school needs to do in order to 'transform' itself from the situation described at B to the one described at C.

Do not interpret the 'next' of the subtitle too literally here. It is necessary to look both to the things the school needs to do immediately and to those which will need doing later on. My reason for using the colloquial 'next steps' phrase is to emphasise the need to consider immediately how the school needs to *act* in order to give life to its strategy. Consideration of this aspect immediately following a review of both the situation now and the intended future has the effect of reintroducing the existing contexts within which the school must act (eg current expectations or demands and available resources – staff expertise and time in particular). These also inevitably contribute to the strategy which the school will follow. This is the nearest we can get to combating what Mintzberg describes as the difficulty of 'predicting discontinuity'. As he says, none of us have the techniques by which we can do that accurately, we can only extrapolate from the present, which is what this step in the process contributes.

The inclusion of the word 'possible' in the subtitle is my clumsy attempt to indicate that it is not the purpose of this step in the process to define implementation plans in detail. All that is required here is an identification of the broad areas of action which will need to be taken so that the purchase these choices place upon the *overall strategy* which emerges may be discerned.

How will we know we are making progress? [E]

It would be possible to interpret this final step simply in the traditional terms of 'success criteria' familiar to anyone who has completed an action plan. In one sense that is not entirely misleading. However, these tend to relate to end-of-process situations, while what is sought here are indicators of progress, identifiable milestones towards the final goal which will show we are still on track.

In particular, seek to identify what sources of data will give you evidence of movement away from the status quo. For instance, if we consider the feature 'Discipline', a possible source of data might be to count the number of referrals to 'higher authority' which are made by staff over a four-week period at present and repeat the count for another four-week period in, say, six months' time.

Finally at this stage it is worth asking, 'Who else needs to know?' Particularly if you have chosen to conduct this analysis on your own or with a small group of colleagues, it is worth asking whether key groups of 'others' are likely to share your view of the here and now, the future and the steps that are suggested by the gap you perceive between those two states.

Even if you have conducted the analysis with a group, there may well be others whose opinions or actions will have a bearing on the strategy. It is the act of capturing these influences which Pedler *et al*. (1988) refer to as interrogations from below.

It is of course open to you to repeat the exercise, either as it stands or in a refined form such as presenting your (or the groups') conclusions from it for consideration by other interested parties such as parents (or pupils?)

Whatever you decide to do, the important thing to remember is that the views and reactions of others will have a significant influence on your chosen strategy.

8

'Back to Deming':
The 14 Points

Given the number of occasions on which I referred to W Edwards Deming in Chapters 4 and 5 it might be considered risky on my part to return to his ideas at this stage. To recommend also one of his most famous contributions to ideas of organisational health and growth as yet another possible approach to the challenge of strategy review and development may be seen as positively foolhardy. However, I make no apologies that his thinking has been, and is, instrumental in developing my own approach to working in support of schools and colleges.

What I will do at this point though is present this contribution from Deming's overall thesis to you in a briefer and more straightforward form than I have employed earlier and leave you to make what use of it you wish. The particular aspect of Deming's work which I am recommending for the purpose of strategy review and development is his 14 points.

Using the 14 Points

Deming's 14 points, taken from his seminal work *Out of the Crisis*, are reproduced as Figure 8.1 immediately following this introductory text. Before leaving you to contemplate these and make of them what use you wish, I wish to place them a little more clearly in the context of Deming's overall thesis and then offer you my own immediate attempts at interpreting them, briefly, in terms of their relevance to the organisational situations found in schools/colleges.

My suggestion is as follows. Visit each of the points in turn and write out first your own interpretation of the point Deming is making and then a summary analysis of the actual systems and structures currently operating in your own school/college as they relate to that particular 'point'.

The aim should be to examine carefully, if at a general level, the evidence of how closely your school measures up to the criteria of organisational effectiveness that are implicit in the 14 points.

This exercise may of course be conducted as an individual piece of analysis or with a group of colleagues (say the senior management team). I have used it successfully in this latter way on several occasions. A simple instrument for launching such a group process is also included here (Figure 8.2). It is assumed

1. Create constancy of purpose toward improvement of product and service, with the aim to become competitive and to stay in business, and to provide jobs.
2. Adopt the new philosophy. We are in a new economic age. Western management must awaken to the challenge, must learn their responsibilities, and take on leadership for change.
3. Cease dependence on inspection to achieve quality. Eliminate the need for inspection on a mass basis by building quality into the product in the first place.
4. End the practice of awarding business on the basis of price tag. Instead, minimise total cost. Move toward a single supplier for any one item, on a long-term relationship of loyalty and trust.
5. Improve constantly and forever the system of production and service, to improve quality and productivity, and thus constantly decrease costs.
6. Institute training on the job.
7. Institute leadership (see Point 12). The aim of supervision should be to help people and machines and gadgets to do a better job. Supervision of management is in need of overhaul, as well as supervision of production workers.
8. Drive out fear, so that everyone may work effectively for the company.
9. Break down barriers between departments. People in research, design, sales and production must work as a team, to foresee problems of production and use that may be encountered with the product or service.
10. Eliminate slogans, exhortations, and targets for the work force, such as asking for zero defects and new levels of productivity. Such exhortations only create adversarial relationships, as the bulk of the causes of low quality and low productivity belong to the system and thus lie beyond the power of the work force.
11a. Eliminate work standards (quotas) on the factory floor. Substitute leadership.
11b. Eliminate management by objective. Eliminate management by numbers, numerical goals. Substitute leadership.
12. Remove barriers that rob the hourly worker of his right to pride of workmanship. The responsibility of supervisors must be changed from sheer numbers to quality.
13. Institute a vigorous programme of education and self-improvement.
14. Put everybody in the company to work to accomplish the transformation. The transformation is everybody's job.

Figure 8.1 *The 14 points (Deming's theory of management)*

that any group to whom it is presented for use will already have received an explanation of Deming's 14 points and the reasons/purposes behind using them in the way described: they also clearly need a copy of the actual 14 points in front of them as they conduct their own analysis. Presented and used in this way, however, both the comparison of the initial 'gradings' accorded to each point by members of the group and the examination of the reasons given for these (from the 'Evidence or examples' column to the right) can lead to interesting insights of the school/college (its current practice, values and possible future intentions) being gathered and explored.

The 14 Points in Context

Deming presents his 14 points as his own summary of the key aspects of organisation management which leaders must address. He also presents elsewhere in his book 'the seven deadly diseases' which 'stand in the way of the transformation' and a further list of 'obstacles' which he sees as less difficult to eradicate than the 'deadly diseases' but which still have to be addressed if complete transformation is to be achieved. The language is picturesque, if not dramatic. However, to Deming the situation he observed required this. Nothing less than a complete transformation of our fundamental beliefs about people and organisations will, in his view, enable organisations to respond to the challenges of the later 20th and, even more so, of the 21st century. The final, keystone, part of his thesis is therefore what he calls 'Profound Knowledge'. In this he sets out his own central beliefs, what he calls 'fundamental truths', the kinds of values and related assumptions which we all have and which we will only act against under extreme provocation or with a near-certain expectation that we will be proved wrong. I have already shared some aspects of this part of his thesis with you earlier. There is not space to delineate more of it here. If you wish to learn more about it I can only recommend you read *Out of the Crisis* yourself or, perhaps better, one of the many books written about Deming's ideas by others. You will recall that I said earlier how difficult it is to penetrate Deming's ideas first just by reading his own summative work.

My Translation of the 14 Points

1. Create constancy of purpose for improvement of product and service

Rather than schools and colleges simply maintaining the status quo, their task is to *continuously improve* the quality of the learning experience (in its broadest sense), which they provide for all their members – the pupils and staff in particular.

2. Adopt the new philosophy

Schools/colleges must understand better the new age in which they are operating and their leaders (governors, principals/heads, other managers) must work on the basis that rapid continuing change is now an integral part of our world and schools/colleges must be planned and run on this basis.

3. Cease dependence on inspection to achieve quality

Schools/colleges, despite Ofsted etc, must learn how to place the monitoring of quality (of the learning experience of the individual pupil) in the hands of the only people who can ensure it is a routine part of their responsibility, ie the teachers. Mutual observation, reflection and analysis between peers organised and enabled by the school's/college's management, is intrinsic to achieving this shift of quality control from the 'end of the line' into the hands of the only people who can do anything effective to achieve the continuous improvement that is sought.

4. End the practice of awarding business on the basis of the price tag

Apart from the obvious relevance for school administrators and others who are ordering supplies and services I find this the most difficult of the 14 points to transcribe in terms of its central relevance to schools/colleges.

However the emphasis which Deming places on establishing long-term relationships based on loyalty and trust speaks of values which all effective educational organisations rightly hold dear.

5. Improve constantly and forever the system of production and service

In some ways a restatement of or development from point 1 in its emphasis on the continuing nature of improvement, this point nevertheless adds the crucial dimension of 'decreasing costs'. To me this speaks of the need for schools/colleges to ensure that the systems they put in place to achieve their objectives are not wasteful – especially of people's time and energies. They need to constantly seek to improve communication, particularly to ensure that those who are 'in charge' can 'hear' what those who are largely responsible for doing the basic job are saying, thinking and feeling. At a more mundane level ensuring that all formal meetings are well conducted – to clear agendas, well chaired, to time and with effective minutes leading to – action is a simple enough check for any school/college to apply to its current ways of working.

6. Institute training on the job

It is essential that managers in schools/colleges ensure that those whose work they are responsible for supporting or supervising are adequately prepared for the work they are expected to do. How many schools in the last few years have suddenly requested 'schemes of work' from their subject co-ordinators or heads of department when there was no established tradition of these in schools, nor any readily available technology through which to acquire them?

Helping people to learn, alongside their job, *how* to do what you expect of them is crucial. In the new contexts of continuing change represented here this, too, is a never-ending responsibility.

7. Institute leadership

Deming's own words almost say it all here. Leadership – inspiring people to follow a shared vision and actively supporting their efforts – should replace more traditional managerial concepts of 'letting them get on with it' and then 'blaming them (even if privately to others rather than directly to them) when things go wrong'.

8. Drive out fear

This point flows naturally from the one above. Where active support towards doing the job better has replaced the allocation of blame for mistakes then fear will be removed. John Cleese, in a speech to the American Institute of Training, observed that a crucial symptom of a healthy organisation is that one asks for forgiveness more often than one asks for permission. In other words schools/colleges must consciously seek to create an ethos where thoughtful experimentation is positively encouraged. In a school/college where people are afraid of making a mistake no one will do any more than they are told to do and many will do less than that.

9. Break down barriers between departments

The organisational culture which this point challenges is so familiar that it hardly needs further extrapolation. The 'feudal baronies' of the subject departments in secondary schools and colleges are one of the most obvious organisational examples of what Deming is challenging here. However even in the primary sector I have observed an almost complete lack of professional colloquy between the infants and the juniors in some schools. And all schools/colleges seem to have their quota of individuals and groups who frequently use the personal pronoun to justify a particular view or position they are holding: my subject, my room, my computer etc.

Schools/colleges should be consciously conceived and managed as *teams* of people in pursuit of the common objective of providing the most effective set of learning opportunities for pupils that they can. The pupil and her or his current learning needs should be the unifying perspective around which teams of teachers pursue the variety of tasks required to meet those needs. 'Our pupils' and 'their learning' should replace 'my subject' etc.

10. Eliminate slogans, exhortations and targets for the workforce

Deming is not railing here against the idea of specified objectives devised to guide groups and individuals towards agreed goals. Schools and colleges are seldom, in my experience, prone to fall into the trap which this point does rage against – of hierarchically defined norms of performance which the organisation expects. Nevertheless I have recently seen a few schools following the example (erroneous in Deming's terms) of business companies in displaying proud, rhetorical claims about what the school stands for and, worse, what everyone reading the notice should do to ensure it happens. I have yet to see any which suggested to me that Deming's advice on this particular front should be ignored.

11. Eliminate work standards and management by objective

Schools/colleges should avoid any tendency – despite (or even perhaps because of) burgeoning league tables – to set numerically calculated targets by which performance will be measured. Energies should be directed to working with staff, and helping them to work with each other, to enable them to set their own standards so that they can constantly develop these. Checking what help they need to do this rather than checking they have done what they have been told (by numerical quota) should characterise how the school's/college's leadership monitors the constant development of the organisation's levels of achievement.

12. Remove barriers that rob people of pride of workmanship.

Schools/colleges should be places where people are encouraged and helped to give of their best. Do any of the current systems actually put constraints in the way of achieving this end? For instance does the allocation of non-teaching time follow logically from a calculation of the total workload of each member of staff? Or is it largely based on status and the associated traditional assumptions about seniority, and possibly even length of service? All of these may be relevant but they, and every other part of the system, should be checked against the criteria provided by this twelfth point.

13. Institute a vigorous programme of education and self-improvement

Schools are often quite good at this, especially since the advent of targeted grants for in-service training, Nevertheless it should be an explicit part of the school's development to draw up a coherent approach to staff training and development which balances the institutional needs with the aspirations and needs of individuals, eg for refreshment, new skills or career enhancement. It is not enough to simply publicise available 'courses' generally and/or wait for individual staff to ask for help in this regard. That is not a 'vigorous' way to respond to this point in Deming terms, and many opportunities to provide for staff development via carefully structured support and challenge inside the school will go missing in such a passive reactive situation.

The training and development of *all* staff is an axiomatic part of Deming's thesis about people in organisations.

14. Put everybody in the company to work to accomplish the transformation

It is the responsibility of the most senior managers and policy makers (including governors) to ensure that the 14 points are addressed. But they can only meet this responsibility by seeking from the outset to involve everybody. This they do through careful explanation, preparation and training, the latter especially in the skills of working together. Every single contribution to the whole must be equally valued. The only way to do this – to achieve the 'transformation' Deming seeks to promote by the 14 points – is to make certain that no one is forgotten and that, though individuals and groups may receive different kinds of support, training and encouragement, all feel that they have a part to play and know (by the routine signs the organisation gives them) that their contribution is valued.

Instructions

1. Read each of the 14 points in turn.
2. Against each point record your assessment of the school/college's current position on the scale (page 111) by quickly ticking the box which best represents *your* experience of working in the organisation: the organisation in this case is the school/college.
3. Now reconsider each item in turn. Don't change your rating but try to call to mind specific examples of 'the way we do things round here' which explain to you why you have ticked the scale where you have. Make a note of any of these which you find particularly telling in relation to the 'point' under review.
4. Compare and discuss your response (ratings and 'examples/evidence') with colleagues who have completed the same exercise. Look for points of particular unanimity or wide differences and listen actively to the fuller description of the 'evidence' that gave rise to the rating. Study of these factors helps to identify the current realities of your school/college and should point the way to its strategic development.

Notes

There is nothing whatsoever to be gained in completing this exercise unless you are honest with yourself. Ticking any scale either at a particular point because you think others might agree with you or because you would not mind others seeing that 'score' is of no value.

   The purpose of the exercise is to examine critically your own perceptions of how the school/college works now as an organisation in terms of Deming's 14 points. All perceptions are valid if they are honestly held and arise from real experience. There are no right or wrong answers in this exercise.

   We all have more to learn by an open comparison of our perceptions – all of which are inevitably and properly linked to the perspectives which our own particular role provides, and to the length of time we have each worked in the school/college.

Figure 8.2 *Analysis exercise based on Deming's 14 points*

Perception of the school/college as a 'Deming organisation'

Deming's point number	Level 1 → I think the school is a good example of this or is good at this already ... Level 6 → I think we have to do a vast amount more on this front before we could be satisfied (Please tick the box on each line below which most appropriately represents your view of the school's/college's position on the above continuum)						'Evidence' or examples (of aspects of the school/college which make you form the judgement you have on each of the continua)
	1	2	3	4	5	6	
1							
2							
3							
4							
5							
6							
7							
8							
9							
10							
11							
12							
13							
14							

9

The End of all Our Exploring

We shall not cease from exploration
And the end of all our exploring
Will be to arrive where we started
And know the place for the first time.

These lines from T S Eliot's *Four Quartets* remind us of the basic truth about all journeys of exploration – that they serve above all to increase our knowledge of ourselves, our values and purposes which give each of us our own personal starting points. That has been my cohering theme in what might otherwise seem to be a random collection of approaches to strategic planning.

Within my understanding of the concept of strategy to ensure at least the possibility of genuinely strategic growth and development it is essential to seek actively ever deeper knowledge of what we, in schools and colleges are about. All organisations face the continual risk that their belief in themselves (which all of us need to sustain us in whatever we are trying to do) will lead them to take what they are doing, and the ways they are doing it, for granted; to assume that this (their present state) is what they are for and how they are meant to be.

Schools and colleges are no different in this respect from other organisations. In fact, the nature of their basic, traditional role – the transmission of knowledge and skills from those who know (the experts or teachers) to those who don't (the inexpert or learners) – makes it likely that they will be especially prone to this risk: certainty and conviction are expected of those who assume the role of the expert.

Faced with this dilemma I believe that schools/colleges, more than any other kind of organisation, need regularly to revisit their starting points. They need to do this of course in order to check that these are still valid in the sense that they meet the needs of the inevitably altered situations which a continually changing world brings about. However, they also need to do this to ensure that their starting points remain authentic in themselves, that they make sense in ways that enable them to explain to others, with complete conviction, what they are doing and why they are doing it. It is my conviction that to achieve this schools and colleges need the kind of knowledge of themselves which Eliot suggested was the outcome of continuous exploration, a conviction which lies behind my earlier explanations of each of the approaches to strategic planning. What I have been seeking to provide is in fact a series of different telescopes through which schools and colleges can explore their own worlds with a view to comprehending them better as a whole within their present and (possible) future contexts. Telescopes rather than microscopes because, in seeking to distil strategy, we need the world-view of our organisations rather than an intimate picture of each of its component parts. And we need that view of our own world from the distance which a telescope lends us.

However, obtaining that distanced and holistic picture of our own organisational world requires us, as Eliot's verses indicate, to attempt the almost impossible task of making an objective, even detached assessment of the beliefs and values which underpin our purposes, while retaining that intimate awareness of immediate (and usually urgent) needs and pressures which our familiarity with our own everyday practice brings. Being able therefore to utilise that familiarity in a way which will provide the insights required for objective reassessment is crucial.

I hope that the approaches to strategic planning which I have set out in preceding chapters have suggested a variety of possible ways in which schools and colleges might be able to obtain this balance between familiarity and detachment and so pursue this 'almost impossible task' with confidence. However, there is one more respected and well-tried theory which I wish to put before you because, perhaps above all others, it provides a powerful framework for the kind of organisational learning needed. It thus supplies me with that cohering element for my own thinking to which I referred above and as such lies behind my own interpretation and use of each of the previous models I have recommended. It is a theory which links ideas about learning specifically to organisations and comes from the work of Chris Argyris and Donald Schön (1974).

Organisational Learning

The basic structure of Argyris and Schön's theory of organisational learning is derived from their observations of and work with individual professional practitioners, and they describe their findings as a 'theory of action'. Summarised briefly they say that all of us develop ideas or thoughts about the way we act or behave in given sets of circumstances.

Even though many of us would not normally grace these with the term 'theory' Argyris and Schön are quite certain they are, because they fulfil all the conditions one would apply to, for instance, a scientific theory. In the form in which we formulate these theories in our head and can explain them to others, Argyris and Schön term these ideas our 'espoused theories'. Any one of our espoused theories therefore is simply the collection of ideas or concepts which provides us with the framework by means of which we intend to determine our actions. So when for instance we set out to arrange a meeting with colleagues, our espoused theory about meetings will determine whether or not we deem an agenda to be important, how we intend to chair the meeting, whether it should result in minutes and so on.

Their theory of action thesis does not stop there however. What their observation of people in work revealed is that the prevailing circumstances tend to affect the way we actually put our espoused theory into action. The result is often a different pattern of actions to that which would have been predicted from our espoused theory. Nevertheless it is still possible to discern the basic construct of ideas which determine the choices of possible alternative actions. Argyris and Schön refer to this as our 'theory in use'. They observe that individuals have a great deal to learn from studying the difference between their own espoused theories and their theories in use (their actual practice). It is for this reason that they, and many other practitioners in the field of adult learning, recommend the routine practice of structured reflection through which one can record the key features of what actually occurred for later comparison with what was intended.

Applying this basic thesis to organisations, Argyris and Schön described how they too work on a combination of espoused theories and theories in use. Examples of a school's espoused theory would be a mission statement, policy statements or the school development plan. Examples of a school's/college's theory in use would be the habitual ways in which staff carry out their work, in particular those parts of their work which can be described as corporate, such as the application of discipline systems or the procedures set down for the marking and assessment of student work

From their work with organisations, Argyris and Schön describe how these different aspects of organisational theories in action are driven by a constantly changing mixture of private images and public maps. Private images are held in the minds and perceptions of individuals of what is supposed to go on (theory espoused) and what is actually going on (theory in use) in the organisation. Public maps are to be found in policy statements and organisation charts (espoused) and in the traditional ways the organisation, in its collective modes of operation, has of going about things which together are referred to by others as the culture of an organisation but which also represent a form of organisational theory in use.

To discover how an organisation learns it is necessary to find ways of decoding this complex mix of private images and public maps, particularly at the level of its organisational theory in use – the prevailing organisational culture. Argyris and Schön point out that most organisations do this by conducting structured reviews of their current practice and performance, which members of the organisation respond to by detecting mismatches between the organisation's desired and actual outcomes. Ways of correcting these are then sought and implemented and the organisation develops, in the sense that it eliminates one or more sources of error and so meets its own objectives more effectively next time. To me this is precisely what the best school development plans do so well. Argyris and Schön call this single-loop learning and recognise its importance in the maintenance and routine improvement of any organisation.

However, the problem concealed in this process is that the members' actions which lead to the correction of the errors are conceived and implemented within the framework of the organisation's current theories in action. Inevitably therefore development takes the form of doing more of the same, only doing it better. If strategic development is sought it is necessary to find a way of learning which will allow the organisation to question and challenge its existing norms of practice, even its sense of fundamental or core purpose. The form of learning which accomplishes this Argyris and Schön call 'double-loop learning'. They describe it as 'those sorts of organisational inquiry which resolve incompatible organisational norms by setting new priorities and weightings of norms, or by restructuring the norms themselves together with associated strategies and assumptions' (1984).

Schools/colleges need therefore consciously to adopt approaches to the review and reassessment of their activities and of their chosen structures and systems which will enable them to engage from time to time in double-loop learning. Only in this way will they achieve that balance between their own inevitable familiarity with their current practice and the objective re-examination of the fundamentals on which these are (or should be) predicated, which is necessary if they are to acquire the holistic, detached picture of themselves required for truly strategic growth.

Conclusions

My hope is that each of the approaches to strategic development which I have described offers the possibility of conducting a double-loop learning process within your school or college.

I have also suggested various levels of application in order to try to accommodate many different preferences for the ways in which they can be used – for individual or group use, from rapid personal brainstorming to the more time-consuming (but more motivating) involvement of a wide range of others.

My claim to coherence is that in every instance I have been guided by the model of organisational learning I have described above. For me, as organisations intrinsically and explicitly involved in learning, schools and colleges can gain not only a strategic purchase on their development but also contribute to the quality of their own achievements by adopting an approach to that development which promotes the capacity for double-loop learning which Argyris and Schön so strongly espouse.

And finally, here is one last model especially for those who were earlier hopeful, when I mentioned Mintzberg's strategic development category of the *visionary* approach, that this book might leave behind its structured, step-by-step approaches in favour of a more broadly creative way of developing strategy. It came to me from the management development director of a major UK industrial company and despite its brevity and simplicity (or perhaps because of it?) offered yet another useful construct, at least for the mental contemplation of strategy. It arose, apparently, as a result of a self-development programme for senior managers which, after its first stage (a three-day residential workshop), looked likely to achieve nothing. It was discovered as the participants were gathering for the second and final workshop three months later that *none* of them had made any real progress with their personal action plans since the first workshop. The result was a challenge from the development director to use the four days of the second workshop to achieve something worthwhile in the locality of their hotel. Each member of the group was given the remainder of the first half-day to research local needs and come up with a project about which she or he was enthusiastic. The group reconvened at lunch time, each member proposed her or his project and the group held a brief discussion from which emerged the three projects which commanded the most support. The group then divided itself into three and joined their respective project leaders – the proposers of each project.

The three groups then had until 9am on day four to complete their projects. At this time they would reconvene as a whole group, report on the level of success of each project group and analyse the process by which success had been achieved. All three projects reached their targets; one (the most ambitious by far) exceeded them. In just over 48 hours a group of four people in a foreign country had raised over £30,000 in cash for a local school for children of the poor (the casualties of the battle for supremacy between church and government schools which then prevailed in that country). They had also arranged for local contractors (at their own expense) to provide a hard-surface play area for the school and repair and decorate the two (ex-army hut) classrooms in which the school operated. They had also appeared on local television with the school's volunteer teacher, a representative of the church authorities and an official of the government, and obtained for the school, in public, promises of continuing support for its work from the two national figures.

Analysis of the processes followed by the three groups and a comparison of these to discover any strong common features resulted in Figure 9.1. This outcome was clearly strongly influenced by the factors which appeared to have enabled the most successful group to achieve what they did, but everyone agreed that wherever success had been achieved most of these factors had been present. This is how they chose to present their conclusions.

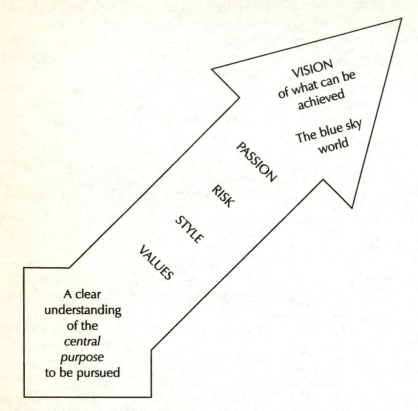

Figure 9.1   *'The sky is the limit' – strategic development powered by vision*

I cannot guess what resonance the figure may have for you as a guide and spur to your thinking about the development of your school or college, but it appealed to me. First by the simplicity with which it captures the essentials of the process of growth. It also fired my imagination through its visual imagery: the solid, four-square base of purpose linked to the upward-pointing arrow of vision by the four key contributing, compelling and organic factors of a clear value system, congruent and appropriate styles of behaviour, the readiness to take risks (particularly with one's own dignity from the examples I heard) and the passion and concomitant conviction needed to see things through.

References

Abbott, R, *et al.* (1988) *Guidelines for the Review and Institutional Development of Schools: School Handbook, Primary and Secondary Versions*, 2nd edn, Schools Curriculum Development Committee (SCDC), Longman, Harlow.

Argyris, C and Schön D (1974) *Theory in Practice*, Jossey-Bass, San Francisco, CA.

Argyris, C and Schön, D (1984) 'What is an organisation that it may learn?' in *Organisations: Case Issues and Concepts*, R Patson *et al.* (eds), Open University, Milton Keynes.

Beavis, A K and Thomas, AR (1996) 'Metaphors as storehouses of expectation', *Educational Management and Administration*, **24**, 1, 99.

Deming, W Edwards (1992) *Out of the Crisis*, Cambridge University Press, Cambridge.

Earley, P (Project Director) (1992) *Standards for School Management*, Project paper published by School Management South.

Foster, G (1989) 'Mintzberg's Strategic Force', *Management Today*, April, 73–6.

Handy, C (1996) 'Handy's View', *Management Today*, November 29.

Hargreaves, D and Hopkins, D (1991) *The Empowered School*, Cassell, London.

Kolb, D (1984) *Experiential Learning: Experience as the source of learning and development*, Prentice-Hall, Englewood Cliffs, NJ.

Morton, D (1994) in *Management Today*, October.

Pedler, M, Burgoyne, J and Boydell, T (1988) 'Learning Company Project Report', Training Agency, Moorfield, Sheffield

Pedler, M, Burgoyne, J and Boydell, T (1991) *The Learning Company*, McGraw-Hill, Maidenhead.

Rhodes, L (1990) 'On the road to equality: Learnings and possibilities', *The School Administrator* (Journal of the American Association of School Administrators), November, 24–34.

Index